"The Christian life is a battle! Spiritual warfare is a reality to be faced, not a concept to be debated. On a topic that is so prone to high extremes, I highly recommend Chip Ingram's biblical and balanced approach that shows us how to recognize, prepare for, and defeat Satan's schemes in our lives."

Howard G. Hendricks, distinguished professor and chairman, Center for Christian Leadership, Dallas Theological Seminary

"My friend Chip has done all of us one big favor. He has reminded us that there is another world . . . a far more important and dangerous world . . . where we do battle every day. Better yet, he has with clarity and candor shown us the way to win the battle in the name of our champion Jesus!"

Dr. Joseph M. Stowell, teaching pastor, Harvest Bible Chapel

"When life seems to hit a brick wall head on . . . or when the brick wall seems to be falling on your life, there may be more than meets the eye. There is a warfare raging, not simply with terrorists across the globe . . . but with spiritual forces for the soul of our culture, our families, and our lives. Chip Ingram deftly and expertly leads us through a biblical boot camp to equip us to stand firm in the battle, and come out on the winning end. This is a handbook I would highly recommend to every Christ follower serious about making life count and living it to the max."

Bob Reccord, president, North American Mission Board

Other books by Chip Ingram

*God: As He Longs for You to See Him*

*Holy Ambition: What It Takes to Make a Difference for God*

*Holy Transformation: What It Takes for God to Make a Difference in You*

*I Am with You Always: Experiencing God in Times of Need*

*Love, Sex, and Lasting Relationships: God's Prescription for Enhancing Your Love Life*

*Sex 180: The Next Revolution* (with Tim Walker)

# The Invisible War

## What Every Believer Needs to Know about Satan, Demons, and Spiritual Warfare

## CHIP INGRAM

**BakerBooks**

Grand Rapids, Michigan

Published by Baker Books
a division of Baker Publishing Group
P.O. Box 6287, Grand Rapids, MI 49516-6287
www.bakerbooks.com

Paperback edition published 2007

ISBN 978-0-8010-6825-6

Published in association with Yates & Yates, LLP, Attorneys and Counselors, Orange, California.

Printed in the United States of America

  The Library of Congress has cataloged the hardcover edition as follows:
Ingram, Chip, 1954–
  The invisible war : what every believer needs to know about satan, demons, and spiritual warfare / Chip Ingram.
    p.  cm.
  Includes bibliographical references.
  ISBN 10: 0-8010-1288-0 (cloth)
  ISBN 978-0-8010-1288-4 (cloth)
  1. Devil—Christianity. 2. Spiritual warfare. I. Title.
BT981.I49 2006
235'.4—dc22                   2005025954

13  14  15  16    13  12

To Fred and Bebe with gratitude beyond what we could ever express for your love and support of Theresa, myself, and all of our children in the midst of our greatest spiritual battles.

Chip

# Contents

# Acknowledgments

It takes a team to do anything of significance in life, and this book is no exception. My thanks to Sealy and Curtis Yates for launching this project; to Vicki Crumpton of Baker Books, who is a joy to work with; and Chris Tiegreen of Walk Thru the Bible, who helped me take tapes, notes, and outlines and make them better and easier to read and understand. Our team's hope is that you will know the truth and the truth will set you free.

# Introduction

The year was 1990. God had made it clear that my time in Texas as pastor of Country Bible Church was coming to an end. We had enjoyed serving in this rural community for eight years. This was where I had learned to be a pastor. I had developed deep foundations and grown personally in this small town, but God was moving us to a new ministry. His direction was very clear for me and my family. But with every turn came the same warning: "Be on your guard, Chip. You are entering an area of fierce spiritual combat, and you need to prepare yourself."

As we interviewed for the job in California, a number of people said this to us in a variety of ways. The elders, key staff members, and specific lay leaders individually welcomed us wholeheartedly, but they also warned us of what we might experience with regard to spiritual warfare. To be honest, I thought they were just a little paranoid. I was a pastor and had dealt with spiritual warfare in ministry before. I had traveled to many countries around the world and seen firsthand the reality of the battle. Besides, God had prepared me with an excellent seminary education—I could exegete Ephesians 6 with the best of them. Or so I thought.

But I began to realize that God was up to something when one of my closest friends and mentors in Texas scheduled a special lunch with me. He was always very discerning and had the habit of regularly fasting and praying for me. I don't remember him ever being more serious than he was at that lunch. "Chip, you are entering a new era in your ministry, and I have the strongest impression from the Lord that you need to prepare yourself for a whole new level of spiritual warfare. I believe God is going to use you in a very significant way, but you will experience spiritual opposition like you've never known before. You need to get ready for the battle."

Those words were prophetic. Our twelve years in Santa Cruz, California, proved to be a graduate course in spiritual warfare. I would come to learn that this town had more satanic bookstores than Boulder, Colorado, a renowned center of occult activity. I would be confronted with the most fearful experiences in my spiritual life. I would live in an environment where the occult, New Age beliefs, and cults were so common that ads on coffee shop bulletin boards included "how to cast spells," "how to contact your spirit guide," and "warlock coven meets 7 p.m. Monday nights."

During those twelve years, we experienced very bizarre—as well as very subtle—spiritual warfare tactics. My intellectual understanding of key Bible passages was woefully inadequate for the issues we were facing. But as I prepared myself in the midst of the battle, I constantly ran into two extremes in the resources I studied. It was easy to find quality biblical information about spiritual warfare that was rooted in the meaning of words, the tense of verbs, and how the armor of God was a metaphor Paul had derived from a Roman soldier. But application was almost nonexistent. There was no real sense of how to use God's truth in the midst of the frightful and often bizarre experiences we were facing.

On the other hand, there was an equally plentiful array of resources that were highly experiential when it came to this subject. They described conversations with demons, extreme manifestations of the spiritual world, and anecdotal answers for which I could find very limited, if any, biblical basis. In fact, some of them made it sound as if the final outcome was still up in the air. While one group of people was virtually ignoring any practical warfare, the other was fighting as though Satan might actually win.

This book is my best attempt to bridge the gap in the teaching available on spiritual warfare. Although it is an exposition of Ephesians 6, the reader will find the application of this passage far from theoretical. When one is ministering in a culture where witches are actively praying against you and a horse's head is placed on a stake across from your church to cast a spell on it, there's no room for platitudes or vague, spiritual answers to pressing, difficult questions.

Much of satanic opposition, however, is extraordinarily subtle and has no dramatic manifestations. For this reason, most of the book will deal with the everyday schemes of the evil one in a forthright, biblical, and relevant manner.

The book has been structured for easy access. My experience with believers is that they have bits and pieces of teaching on spiritual warfare, but they have a difficult time putting the pieces together and knowing how to apply them. As a result the book is divided into four sections:

Spiritual Warfare 101—What Every Believer Needs to Know
Spiritual Warfare 201—How to Prepare Yourself for Spiritual Battle

Spiritual Warfare 301—How to Do Battle with the Enemy and Win
Spiritual Warfare 401—Deliverance from Demonic Influence

At the beginning of each section, you will find the biblical text to be studied, an overview, a preview of what the section will cover, an outline, and a reference key to biblical passages for easy review. This will allow the reader a quick overview of the content of each section and provide a ready reference for dealing with spiritual warfare issues in the future. Preachers, teachers, and Bible students may find this material most helpful. Some readers may prefer to dive right into the chapters, but I hope many will use this outline and the content of this book to systematically apply the truth of God's Word on this subject in a way that will break strongholds in their lives. As I've had the privilege of teaching this material around the country, I have seen firsthand what God can and will do when we understand our position in Christ, put on the full armor of God, and know what it looks like to stand firm, "taking every thought captive to the obedience of Christ" (2 Cor. 10:5).

The chapters within each section, however, will follow a more traditional pattern of teaching, using illustrations and suggesting relevant uses in the reader's life. My hope is to provide a resource to the body of Christ that will be warm, personal, biblically accurate, interesting, and, most of all, spiritually helpful; and, at the same time, be structured in a way to prove valuable as a timeless resource for those who teach, counsel, or find themselves in environments where a systematic, clear, and practical reference is needed.

My prayer is that God will use this material to help you know the truth that will set you free—"for greater is He who is in you than he who is in the world" (1 John 4:4).

# Spiritual Warfare 101

## What Every Believer Needs to Know

There are two equal and opposite errors into which our race can fall about the devils. One is to disbelieve in their existence. The other is to believe, and to feel an excessive and unhealthy interest in them.

C. S. Lewis

Finally, be strong in the Lord and in the strength of His might. Put on the full armor of God, so that you will be able to stand firm against the schemes of the devil. For our struggle is not against flesh and blood, but against the rulers, against the powers, against the world forces of this darkness, against the spiritual forces of wickedness in the heavenly places.

Ephesians 6:10–12

## Introduction: Opening Your Eyes

In this central New Testament passage about spiritual warfare, Paul tells his readers the nature of the battle and how they are to fight it. This first section—Spiritual Warfare 101—will cover Paul's general command in verse 10, his specific command in verse 11, and the reason he gives in verse 12 for both commands. As we move on through the passage, we will discover five basic truths to ground us in the reality of the invisible war and to guide us in our thinking.

### The General Command—"Be strong in the Lord, and in the strength of His might" (v. 10)

The full meaning of this command is captured in this expanded translation: "Allow yourself to be continually strengthened by the power already made available to you in your new position and relationship with Christ." It is the power that raised Jesus from the dead and now dwells in you.

### The Specific Command—"Put on the full armor of God" (v. 11)

How do you allow yourself to be strong in the Lord? By continually and repeatedly putting on the spiritual protection God has provided for you at specific points in time, for the express purpose of holding on to your position in Christ as you are bombarded by satanic strategies designed to destroy you or render you ineffective in kingdom pursuits.

### The Reason for the Commands—"Our struggle is not against flesh and blood" (v. 12)

Our real struggle—our battle, our wrestling match to the death—is not against physical or material adversaries like people, circumstances, and organizations. It is against a hierarchy of demonic forces doing battle in the spiritual realm.

## Five Basic Truths about Spiritual Warfare

1. *There is an invisible world.*
   The invisible world is just as real as the visible world, and both Old and New Testaments refer to it often.
   a. 2 Kings 6:15–19: Elisha, surrounded by a hostile army, tells his servant that invisible hosts are protecting them.
   b. Daniel 10: An angel reveals to Daniel the battle he has been waging.
   c. Ephesians 6:12: One of many references by Paul to a conflict that is not of the flesh.

2. *We are involved in an invisible war.*
   This cosmic conflict has eternal implications; lives are at stake. The enemy's strategies affect us every day. When was the last time you honestly considered that some struggle or relational conflict was rooted in satanic opposition?
   a. 2 Corinthians 10:3–5: "Though we walk in the flesh, we do not war according to the flesh, for the weapons of our warfare are not of the flesh, but divinely powerful for the destruction of fortresses. We are destroying speculations and every lofty thing raised up against the knowledge of God, and we are taking every thought captive to the obedience of Christ."
   b. 2 Corinthians 4:4: "The god of this world has blinded the minds of the unbelieving so that they might not see the light of the gospel of the glory of Christ, who is the image of God."

3. *Our foe is formidable.*
   The goal of Satan is to destroy God's people and discredit the cause of Christ. He is not to be taken lightly. He is real. He was an angel, the highest of all created beings, who rebelled against God out of pride.
   a. 1 Peter 5:8: "Be of sober spirit, be on the alert. Your adversary, the devil, prowls about like a roaring lion, seeking someone to devour."

b. Jude 9: "Michael the archangel, when he disputed with the devil and argued about the body of Moses, did not dare pronounce against him a railing judgment, but said, 'The Lord rebuke you!'"

c. Is Satan for real?
  - the authority of the Bible: Genesis 3:1; 1 Chronicles 21:1; Revelation 12:9
  - the testimony of Christ: Matthew 4:1–11; also Christ refers to Satan twenty-five times
  - the reality of demons: Satan is their "prince" (Luke 11:15)

d. Who is Satan?
  - a created spirit: Job 1:6; Colossians 1:16
  - an angel: Matthew 25:41; Revelation 12:7
  - a cherub: Ezekiel 28:14
  - the highest of all created beings: Ezekiel 28:14

e. Where did he come from?
  - created perfect: Ezekiel 28:12–13
  - had a heavenly estate: Jude 6
  - a guardian of God's glory: Ezekiel 28:14
  - the occasion of his sin = power and beauty: Ezekiel 28
  - the nature of his sin = pride: Isaiah 14:13; 1 Timothy 3:6
  - the cause of his sin = personal, free choice: Habakkuk 1:13; James 1:13

4. *We must respect our foe but not fear him.*
Our responsibility is to become acutely aware of Satan's methods but not be preoccupied by them. We can become educated about his schemes by examining his names in Scripture; all of them reveal something of his tactics. Scripture is very clear about his agenda and his targets. But he is limited, and we have no need to fear him if we follow God's instructions in faith.

a. 2 Corinthians 2:11: Paul agrees to forgive a brother along with the Corinthian church—in order that "no advantage would be taken of us by Satan, for we are not ignorant of his schemes."

b. The vital question: how can we make sure we are not ignorant of his schemes?
  *Satan's names reveal his tactics.*
  - Satan (adversary): Job 1:6–7; 1 Thessalonians 2:18
  - Devil (slanderer): 1 Peter 5:8
  - Lucifer (son of the morning): Isaiah 14:12

- Beelzebub (lord of the flies): Matthew 12:24
- Belial (a false god): 2 Corinthians 6:15
- Evil one: 1 John 5:19
- Tempter: 1 Thessalonians 3:5
- Prince of this world: John 12:31 (NIV)
- Accuser of the brethren: Revelation 12:10
- Representations include:
    Serpent: Genesis 3
    Dragon: Revelation 12
    Angel of light: 2 Corinthians 11:14

*Satan attacks God's program, the church, by*:
- False philosophies: Colossians 2:8
- False religions: 1 Corinthians 10:20
- False ministers: 2 Corinthians 11:14–15
- False doctrine: 1 John 2:18
- False disciples: Matthew 13:24–30
- False morals: 2 Thessalonians 2:7–12

*Satan attacks God's people by*:
- Directing governments: Daniel 10:13
- Deceiving people: 2 Corinthians 4:4
- Destroying lives: Hebrews 2:14
- Persecuting the saints: Revelation 2:10
- Preventing service: 1 Thessalonians 2:18
- Promoting schisms: 2 Corinthians 2:10–11
- Planting doubt: Genesis 3:1–5
- Producing sects and cults: 1 Timothy 4:1
- Provoking sin:
    Anger: Ephesians 4:26–27
    Pride: 1 Timothy 3:6
    Worry: Matthew 13:22
    Self-reliance: 1 Chronicles 21:1
    Discouragement: 1 Peter 5:6–8
    Worldliness: 1 John 2:16
    Lying: Acts 5:3
    Immorality: 1 Corinthians 5:1–2

*Satan's power is limited.*

Balance and wisdom are crucial in our assessment of spiritual opposition. To assign too much or too little credit to the reality of demonic activity is to err greatly.

- He is created, therefore not omniscient or infinite.
- He can be resisted by the Christian: James 4:7.
- God places limitations on him: Job 1:12.

5. *We do not fight* for *victory; we fight* from *victory.*

   As believers in Christ, we are invincible. The Bible has given us numerous promises of victory over the power of the enemy.

   a. 1 John 4:4: "You are from God, little children, and have overcome them; because greater is He who is in you than he who is in the world."

   b. 1 John 5:4–5: "Whatever is born of God overcomes the world; and this is the victory that has overcome the world—our faith. Who is the one who overcomes the world, but he who believes that Jesus is the Son of God?"

   c. Revelation 12:11: "They overcame him because of the blood of the Lamb and because of the word of their testimony, and they did not love their life even when faced with death."

   d. James 4:7: "Submit therefore to God. Resist the devil and he will flee from you."

## Personal Application
_What You Need to Remember_

**1. Satan is a defeated foe.**

"Now judgment is upon this world; now the ruler of this world will be cast out" (John 12:31).

**2. Jesus destroyed the works of the devil.**

"[Jesus] canceled out the certificate of debt consisting of decrees against us, which was hostile to us; and He has taken it out of the way, having nailed it to the cross. When He had disarmed the rulers and authorities, He made a public display of them, having triumphed over them through Him" (Col. 2:14–15).

**3. We are victors in Christ.**

"'O death, where is your victory? O death, where is your sting?' The sting of death is sin, and the power of sin is the law; but thanks be to God, who gives us the victory through our Lord Jesus Christ" (1 Cor. 15:55–57).

**4. We have the power and resources to resist Satan and demonic attacks.**

"You are from God, little children, and have overcome them; because greater is He who is in you than he who is in the world" (1 John 4:4).

**5. We must learn how to put on the full armor of God to experience in daily living the victory we already possess.**

"Therefore, take up the full armor of God, so that you will be able to resist in the evil day, and having done everything, to stand firm. Stand firm therefore, having girded your loins with truth, and having put on the breastplate of righteousness, and having shod your feet with the preparation of the gospel of peace; in addition to all, taking up the shield of faith with which you will be able to extinguish all the flaming arrows of the evil one. And take the helmet of salvation, and the sword of the spirit, which is the word of God" (Eph. 6:13–17).

# 1

# Why You Struggle

> Life is a hard fight, a struggle, a wrestling with the principle
> of evil, hand to hand, foot to foot. Every inch of the way is
> disputed.
>
> Florence Nightingale

The warnings God gave me through friends, mentors, and leaders at Santa Cruz Bible Church were not in vain. Within a year, a number of incidents occurred that let me know we were certainly in a spiritual struggle.

I'll never forget preaching on a Sunday night and hearing bizarre sounds coming from the back of the auditorium. Soon there were more than strange sounds. A man was walking down the aisle as he shouted and screamed. At first I continued to speak, hoping the ushers would be able to handle the situation. But as he walked toward me, our eyes met. I saw a wildness that I can't quite describe. He not only disrupted the service and my message, but he made a scene that only those who witnessed it could believe. What shocked me was how unsurprised the people in the church were.

Apparently this had happened before. Three or four ushers got to this man before he got to me, and I was informed later in a debriefing session that this individual, as far as they could tell, was demonized. Blasphemies against God, the church, and my message spewed from his mouth that night, and it took three or four men to restrain him and usher him out of the auditorium. If I didn't believe in spiritual warfare before, I certainly did now. I got an introduction I would never forget.

That's just one example among many of the reality of the invisible war. You'll read a lot of examples in this book that come from my time in Santa Cruz, simply because the invisible war is so much more visible there. But it's raging everywhere else on this planet too. It may be behind the scenes—in fact, it probably is—but in your house, your church, and your community there is a violent conflict between kingdoms. We're on the winning side, but we have to be aware of the fight. We have to understand spiritual warfare.

Ephesians 6:10–20 is the central teaching in the entire New Testament on spiritual warfare, and it begins with two commands: "Be strong in the Lord," and, "Put on the full armor of God."

### The General Command: "Be strong in the Lord and in the strength of His might" (v. 10)

People who suddenly find out that they are in the midst of a cosmic conflict often have one of two extreme reactions: fight or flight. Those who flee do so because they don't feel up to the task. Those who are ready to jump into the fight do so because they feel strong enough to handle it. Ephesians 6 has an answer to both extremes: be strong in the strength of *God's* might.

We may not know much about this battle when we first realize it exists, but we can at least know that it's not about our ability to muster up our own strength. That's good news if you want to avoid the battle because of your own weakness; your strength (or lack of it) isn't really the issue. And it's also good news if you have the urge to rush into battle under your own abilities; you won't have to run from it when you realize how overpowered you are. There is power available, and it's the greatest power in the universe. The only way to win this war is to be strong in the Lord—in the strength that Paul spent most of Ephesians assuring us is already ours.

This general command to be strong in God's power applies to every believer at all times. Note that word *command*. This is not optional for a Christian. There is nothing in this passage or in the New Testament to indicate that we can dismiss ourselves from the battle—not without suffering great harm or missing out on substantial blessings. Grammatically, this instruction is in the present imperative tense and the passive voice. That means it's an order and a matter of obedience, yet it's a passive obedience—something we have to allow someone else to do for us.

If I were to paraphrase this verse, it would look something like this: "Allow yourselves to be continually strengthened by the power already available to you in your new position and relationship with Christ." And if we were to dig into the meaning of *power*, we would find that it is the Greek word from which we get *dynamite*. This is the same power that raised Jesus from the dead and now dwells in us. That may take a while to sink in, but it needs to. That's the basis for winning this battle. Our churches, our families, our relationships, and our work lack something absolutely crucial if we miss this. We need to allow God to develop our lives in such a way that the power made available to us in our new relationship with him gives us the strength to win.

## The Specific Command: "Put on the full armor of God" (v. 11)

The second command tells us how to fulfill the first one. It is a specific command. We are to put on the full armor of God for the purpose of standing firm—or literally, holding our ground. How? By continually and repeatedly putting on the spiritual protection God has given us.

The verb in this command is a little different from the verb in the first command. The tense refers to a specific point in time, and it has a sense of urgency. We don't have time to consider carefully whether we want to be in this war; we are in it whether we acknowledge it or not. This verb also implies something we do for ourselves—there's nothing passive about it. We don't wait for God to do this for us, and we don't do this once and think we never have to do it again. This lifestyle of putting on the armor implies consistent and multiple efforts. We live this way because of what can happen if we don't: relinquishing the benefit of our position in Christ as we are bombarded by schemes designed to destroy us and render us ineffective in kingdom pursuits.

This is not an add-on only for the deluxe-model Christian. Those schemes affect everyone. They are orchestrated in order to tempt us, deceive us, draw us away from God, fill our hearts with half-truths and untruths, and lure us into pursuing good things in the wrong way, at the wrong time, or with the wrong person. The English word *strategies* is derived from the Greek word Paul uses that is translated "schemes." That means our temptations are not random. The false perspectives we encounter do not come at us haphazardly. The lies we hear, the conflicts we have with others, the cravings that consume us when we are at our weakest points—they are all part of a plan to make us casualties in the invisible war. They are organized, below-the-belt assaults designed to neutralize the very people God has filled with his awesome power.

### The Reason for the Commands: "Our struggle is not against flesh and blood" (v. 12)

The Ephesians weren't living in a vacuum. There's a reason Paul gave them these instructions. They may have been having some relationship issues or negative circumstances—they may have even been undergoing intense persecution from government authorities or worshippers of pagan gods and goddesses, for all we know—but that's not why Paul urges them to be strong and put on their armor. The real issue, he says, is behind the scenes. They are in an intense, to-the-death wrestling match with supernatural, evil beings.

That's what his word *struggle* really means. It's a hand-to-hand combat practiced in ancient Greece in which two people would fight until one could hold the other person down. It required constant exertion and concentration. When Paul uses the word in Ephesians, he makes it clear that he's not writing about their outward circumstances or about people. The battle may have been manifesting itself in circumstances, city policies, oppression, and evil behavior, but the source was not flesh and blood. The battle is "against the powers, against the world forces of this darkness, [and] against the spiritual forces of wickedness in heavenly places" (v. 12). It's an *invisible* war.

This list of spiritual powers has connotations of hierarchy and organization. Just as there are generals, privates, and a lot of ranks between them in our military structures, demonic powers also seem to be arranged according to role and power. I've heard people get much more detailed about demonic activity than the Bible ever does, delineating specific hierarchies and describing specific domains of various demons. These are interesting speculations, but they are only speculations; Scripture doesn't spell these things out for us. But even though the Bible doesn't tell us how these vast structures function, it does acknowledge the existence of these evil adversaries doing battle in the spiritual realm, and it is very clear on this point: this is where our fight is.

Many people in the twenty-first century might step back at this point and question the validity of this worldview. After all, it does sound a little weird in a modern, scientific age. If you were to say something in a public gathering about the devil and demons, you would know to brace yourself for incredulous stares and laughter. You might not be taken very seriously. But the Ephesians would have had no such reservations. They had seen demonic power. It was a very common observation. The question for them—and for us, if we embrace the biblical worldview—was not whether evil entities were real but what to do about them. Paul was teaching the Ephesians a God-given strategy for dealing with something they already knew was true.

Our sophisticated worldview can actually hinder us in the situations we confront. We start thinking that the problem is a spouse, a child, a boss, a policy, an illness, or a circumstance. These symptoms are easy to see, and I certainly wouldn't imply that they are never relevant. But they are often just symptoms, not the source of the problem. Behind many of the things we see on the surface is an archenemy who wants to destroy our lives.

Please don't misunderstand this point of view as a denial of personal responsibility. We all make choices. Sometimes the consequences are bad. We can't blame all difficulties on hostile acts of the enemy. We live in a fallen world, and bad things happen. Not everything occurs because of demonic schemes. But everything *can* be exploited by demonic forces. As C. S. Lewis said, the danger is to put either way too much emphasis on Satan and demons or way too little. For most people today, it's way too little.

The fact is, you are going to be assailed. You will have to withstand the onslaughts of the enemy of God. Paul warned us that it would be a rough ride, so fasten your seat belt and focus on your role. Your first responsibility is to be aware of the battle, your second responsibility is to depend on God's strength, and your third responsibility is to use the protection God has provided.

## Personal Application: What about You?

Some people are comfortable with the issues we've discussed to this point. For others, the idea of demonized people blustering up the center aisle of a church or of demonic voices coming from a seemingly normal guy raises some eyebrows. Many of us don't encounter such manifestations in our churches and communities, and a lot of people are pretty sure there's a better explanation than demons. But I can assure you that there are some things that psychology, sociology, and biology can't explain. There are spiritual realities that every believer will either face up to or be defeated by, and only a solid understanding of our spiritual armor can prepare us for those realities.

Before we get into the value of the spiritual armor, however, there are five basic truths we need to be sure we firmly believe. Understanding the role of God's protection will not help us very much if we don't first understand exactly why we need it. If your eyes are not yet open to the behind-the-scenes context of our new life in Christ—if you are still skeptical about the whole business—prepare to be jolted by the reality of the conflict raging around you.

**In Your Life**

- Have you ever sensed that you were in a spiritual battle? If so, when?
- When someone says "spiritual warfare," what immediately comes to your mind?
- What is your natural tendency in a conflict—to fight or to flee?
- Does this tendency undermine God's strength in your life? If so, how?
- Have you ever considered that a besetting sin or an unresolved conflict could in any way be related to spiritual warfare?
- How does it help you to know that the power residing in you is the same power of God that raised Jesus from the dead?

# 2

# Your Life—Behind the Scenes

Millions of spiritual creatures walk the earth unseen, both
when we sleep and when we awake.

John Milton

Normally, we Ingrams sleep through the night like everyone else.
Occasionally, in Santa Cruz, we wouldn't. And when we didn't, it was
often for very frightening reasons.

It's terrifying to have physical manifestations of evil in your home.
Audio manifestations were not uncommon. One night we heard vivid
sounds that could not have been artificial, and then we heard, one by
one, our children crying out with outlandish, satanic nightmares. I can't
describe how terrifying it was. We had to learn as a family that we were
being attacked, and the goal was to make us feel powerless and afraid.
I was tempted to pack up and leave the church, Santa Cruz, and maybe
even the ministry until I realized that Satan's bullets were no match for
God's protection. We had to teach each of our children the basics of
spiritual warfare so they would know what to do in the middle of the
night. We learned that the precision and power of God's spoken Word,
because of his authority and the power of his name, will dispel any of
the enemy's scare tactics—usually immediately, but always eventually.

That may be an extreme example of confronting the invisible world
for most of us, but I recently taught this material to a thousand pastors in Nigeria who didn't even blink when I shared some of my more
terrifying experiences. In fact, they said that in that animistic culture,

nearly everyone had experiences with demons. There is a realm of reality that we can't see in my house or yours, where the real battles of life take place. There's a lot going on behind the scenes.

## Basic Truth #1: There Is an Invisible World

Prime time seemed innocent enough in the sixties when we watched shows like *Bewitched*. The context in that show was a traditional family situation, and there was nothing startling or offensive about the story lines. They usually even contained uplifting moral lessons. The fact that there were witches and warlocks and an entire world of unseen (or disguised) supernatural beings could be chalked up to fantasy. After all, this was simply entertainment.

But have you seen how it grew from there? In the last few years we've been able to watch a supernaturally gifted high-school girl vanquish dark, demonic entities of the underworld in *Buffy the Vampire Slayer*. Audiences have been entertained by an attractive trio of witches who rely on occult incantations to defeat demons and challenge the source of evil in *Charmed*. Shows like *Angel* and *The X-Files* all have cosmic implications. And that's just a sampling from television. Movies, from comic to horror to everything in between, have featured supernatural themes even more prominently: *The Exorcist*, *The Omen*, *Poltergeist*, *Ghoulies*, *Interview with the Vampire*, *The Devil's Advocate*, *The Mummy*, and *The Sixth Sense*, for a few examples among hundreds. Literature is even more full of the occult. Our culture has become fascinated with the ultimate conflict between good and evil, not only in its outward manifestations, but also in the dynamics of the underworld and the spiritual beings who inhabit it. Many viewers see these dynamics as pure fantasy. Many do not.

I would be the first to tell you that the way the invisible world is represented in these various forms of entertainment is, in most cases, pure fantasy. But I would also be the first to tell you that the reality from which these fantasies arise is rock-solid, biblical truth. Whether gifted sophomores can slay vampires is not a scriptural question. Whether evil entities exist and interact with human history is answered emphatically in the Bible, and the answer is *yes*. There is an invisible world, and it's very, very real.

That is "basic truth number one" that we desperately need to be convinced of before we study the scriptural teaching on spiritual warfare: *there is an invisible world that is just as real as the visible world* (Eph. 6:12). The Bible doesn't inform us of this invisible world in passing references or isolated verses here and there. The witness is resounding and pervasive. If the spiritual world of angels and demons is not reality, neither is the Bible. The context of the invisible world in Scripture is just that emphatic. It can't be rationalized out of the Word.

## The Old Testament Witness of the Invisible World

The evil king of Aram was determined to find Elisha and kill him (2 Kings 6:8–14). God would often reveal to Elisha the enemy's plans, and then Elisha would warn the king of Israel. For Aram, it was worse than having a spy in the camp. "[He] tells the king of Israel the words that you speak in your bedroom," one adviser told the king (v. 12). The raids against Israel could never succeed as long as Elisha prophesied. Elisha had to go.

But Elisha had proven elusive. The king of Aram had never been able to trap him, and he was growing more and more frustrated. The only way to exploit Israel, it seemed, was to treat Elisha as the threat that he was. Aram gathered its army.

One morning, Elisha's servant woke up at sunrise and went outside. Surrounding the city of Dothan were hundreds, maybe thousands, of horses, chariots, and warriors. They had come to this city with one goal, and Elisha—sound asleep inside—was the target. The servant panicked and wakened his master. When Elisha assessed this dire situation, he offered one of the strangest statements in all of Scripture: "Do not fear, for those who are with us are more than those who are with them" (2 Kings 6:16).

Elisha's servant must have thought the old man had lost his mind. His prophecies may have been great, but his math was terrible. These two men were completely encircled by a vast army of professional killers, each zealous to satisfy the command of an evil king. The prophet and his attendant were prepared for breakfast, not war. If ever a situation was hopeless, this was it. And Elisha calmly assured the young man that the two of them had the upper hand.

As the story unfolds, we see what Elisha meant. He prayed that his servant's eyes would be opened to the reality of God's army. When the attendant's eyes saw the usually unseen world, he was amazed. Behind Aram's bloodthirsty army on the hills surrounding Dothan were horses and chariots of fire—God's heavenly forces ready to fight supernaturally for the servants of God. For a moment, the invisible became visible, and it was incredible.

For the enemy, the reverse was true; the visible suddenly became invisible. Elisha prayed blindness upon them, and when God answered, the prophet led the hostile army straight to the king of Israel and his forces,

33

where the invaders were immediately captured. The invisible world turned out to be just as real as the visible world—and more powerful.

A fascinating story in Daniel 10 demonstrates the connection between the visible and invisible. Daniel had been praying intensely for three weeks when he had a vision of a powerful angel. This angel told Daniel that his prayer had been heard from day one, but the "prince of the kingdom of Persia" had been resisting the angel in the spiritual realm. The breakthrough came when Michael the archangel came to join the battle (Dan. 10:12–13).

Is Daniel just using figurative language in this passage? There's no indication of that. This vision is too specific and too real to be considered a metaphor. Daniel could hardly breathe when he saw the vision. The people around him were overwhelmed and fled. The prophecies given concerned historic details that were more than symbolic. There is nothing figurative about this glimpse of the invisible world. To Daniel—and to believers ever since—this passage is undeniably real.

These are two ancient stories among others from the Old Testament (2 Kings 6:8–23 and Daniel 10), and they illustrate a point made repeatedly in Scripture: there's a lot going on that we don't see.

## The New Testament Witness of the Invisible World

Belief in the invisible world is not confined to Old Testament times. After the world had grown intellectually sophisticated through complex Greek philosophies and during the age of Roman political and social modernization, the New Testament refers to spiritual realities again and again. Today we tend to look down on earlier eras as naïve and uninformed, but these were fairly advanced cultures that, in spite of being prescientific, were intellectually strong and rigorous in their pursuit of knowledge. New Testament times were not the Dark Ages. Many Greeks and Romans, for example, were just as suspicious of the resurrection as skeptics are today. Why? Because they didn't believe the evidence for it. They were wrong on that point, of course, but we can't accuse them of being gullible. They approached life with reason. The context behind Jesus's ministry and the early church was one of history's most culturally advanced societies.

The rationalism of Greco-Roman culture did not rule out the reality of invisible spirits. There was too much evidence. In that intellectual context, Paul wrote of the difference between the flesh and the spiritual fortresses behind the scenes in 2 Corinthians 10:3–5. The weapons we use are not of the flesh, the battle we fight is not of the flesh, and the thoughts and speculations infiltrating society and the church are not of the flesh. The issues faced by believers are not simply a matter of psychology or socialization, they are not random accidents, and they are not fully explainable by organizational dynamics or relational theories. They are spiritual, and the forces behind them are personal.

Paul referred to these forces repeatedly, writing of the god of this world who has blinded the minds of the unbelieving, of the schemes of the enemy to create bitterness and division in the church, of Satan's ability to hinder him from visiting a particular city, and of the demonic influences behind the persecution he and others faced. John wrote of Satan and demons frequently in his gospel and letters, even concluding his first letter with the observation that "the whole world lies in the power of the evil one" (1 John 5:19). The revelation John received of the cosmic conflict and the end-times was full of references to the dragon and evil spirits. Those beings were embodied in governments and false religious systems, perhaps, but the spiritual reality behind those governments and religious systems was personal and active. Peter wrote to a persecuted group of believers and told them that the devil was prowling around to devour them. Luke recorded the apostles' numerous confrontations with their opposition, and the words coming out of their mouths were pointed and precise: Satan and his demons are behind unbelief, deception, fear, false religions, and persecution. There is no hint in the works of these inspired, God-appointed writers that evil is impersonal and that phenomena can be naturally explained. Their descriptions of encounters with the unseen world are very concrete.

It is important for us to remember that the words of the apostles and inspired writers of the New Testament came out of the context of their encounters with Jesus. They didn't make these things up. The Son of God himself had personal interaction with Satan and demons, and he referred to their work frequently. Many of his miracles were in response to their lies and destruction. He had no reservations about accusing false teachers of satanic influence. The Son of God who came to us from an eternal dwelling—where everything is crystal clear to an omniscient Father—spoke specifically and repeatedly of dark, spiritual personalities. The invisible world was very visible to him.

The implications of the biblical witness are more vital than we might think. These numerous references from Jesus mean that if we don't believe in the invisible world, we are rejecting the words of God's Son and considering him a naïve product of his age. We are saying that the inspired writings of the early church leaders are not very inspired. In trying to reconcile a naturalistic worldview with the Bible, we are sacrificing huge portions of God's truth. If we deny the reality of Satan, demons, and angels, we are casting judgment on the Holy Spirit's revelation to us.

Three centuries after the Enlightenment, we may have a hard time accepting the reality of invisible beings. We explain the Bible's teaching on this subject as the best explanation premodern people could give for some of the things they observed. We don't trust ancient witnesses, and we dismiss today's witnesses as out of touch with reality. We're modern people who rely on empiricism and the scientific method. We like to be able to explain everything by testing and measuring.

For believers in Jesus—people who really believe he is the Son of God—we have to admit that there's a world we can't directly observe. That's the testimony he gave us. He didn't refer to demons in the abstract. They spoke to him and he spoke back. That tells us that this unseen realm is just as real as touching your skin, as real as kissing your children on the cheek when you tuck them in, as real as the back pain you feel after getting rear-ended, and as real as watching a beautiful sunset.

If that's still hard to swallow, consider the multitude of examples we've had throughout history of unseen realities—things that skeptics dismissed because their eyes couldn't see them. For centuries, people couldn't see bacteria, but did that make them less real? What about viruses? Most of us don't thoroughly understand electricity, and we can't really observe electric currents, but is electricity real? We see the evidence of its existence in the tools of our daily lives. We moved beyond our uncertainty of its existence long ago. We can't see natural gas, but if I turn on a valve and light a match at my house, I get heat. We can't see or smell carbon monoxide—it's completely hidden from our senses. But if you stay in a room with enough of it, it will kill you. We can't see the wind, sound waves, or atoms, but they all exist. We can see the results they produce—we know these things are real because we have learned to observe their effects. Historically and even today, there are all kinds of things going on that we can't see. It shouldn't be that hard to accept that there is also a spiritual world we can't see.

Francis Schaeffer wrote a book long ago that had a great impact on me. It was called *True Spirituality*, and it made the point that there is a certain content that fits in the material world—flesh and blood, trees and flowers, the sky and planets—and a parallel content that fills the spiritual world—souls, angels, demons, and all sorts of activity among them. Schaeffer suggested that there is an arch, a connection, between these two realities.[1] We live in that connection.

I don't know exactly how that side of reality works. I have heard some teach in great detail about territorial spirits and how these things operate in the invisible world and affect us. But in Scripture God chose to reveal only a limited understanding of all the specifics of hierarchies and parameters of authority, and as we will see, that is all we need to know. The Bible is very clear about the existence of angels, Satan, and demons and that they are organized by role, power, and rank. We may not know all the details, but we do know what the Bible affirms, and believers cannot realistically dismiss the truths stated in Scripture without dismissing Scripture itself.

We need to understand the biblical dynamics of spiritual realities. If we don't, we will make ourselves more vulnerable to evil powers. We will also be much less confident in God's ability to deliver us. That's essentially what Elisha told his servant in that story from 2 Kings—that he was missing the truth. Just as we tend to do, the servant was looking at circumstances and depending on what his eyes could tell him, completely oblivious to the greater reality behind the visible reality. Elisha said, "I'll give you a glimpse of what you can't see—the unlimited power totally available to us in this moment. Your perspective is wrong, and it's going to change."

The truth is that there is an invisible world that is just as real as the visible world. There are vast numbers of angels, both good and bad—spirits that exist all around us. There are glorious beings that would take our breath away if we saw them, and there are evil beings that would horrify us if we could see them. When Elisha prayed, his servant got a glimpse of what is normally invisible, and the scene was crowded with God's armies available for their protection.

**Personal Application: What about You?**

I wonder how often we believers really look at our own circumstances like Elisha's servant did, completely unaware that there is a lot happening around us that we can't see. It's easy for us to forget that there is more going on behind the scenes. That is why this truth is so important. When we think we can see all there is to see, we get discouraged and depressed, weighed down by circumstances that we can't envision ever changing, and we don't employ the tools God has given us to overcome. When that's the case, according to the testimony of God's Word, we don't have the right perspective. Our eyes aren't really open.

**Basic Truth #2: We Are Involved in an Invisible War**

Not only is there an invisible world, that world is in the midst of an invisible conflict. Basic truth number two is essential for us to understand: *we are involved in an invisible war, a cosmic conflict that has eternal implications* (Eph. 6:12). It is real, it is serious, and it is ultimate in its consequences. We are soldiers in the battle that matters most.

The fact that we were born into the middle of a war raging in the invisible world is not comforting news, but it is vital information. It impacts nearly every area of our lives and, in fact, is the real arena in which we live. Paul's specific teaching in 2 Corinthians 10:3–5 is this: "Though we walk in the flesh, we do not war according to the flesh, for the weapons of our warfare are not of the flesh, but divinely powerful for the destruction of fortresses. We are destroying speculations and every lofty thing raised up against the knowledge of God, and we are taking every thought captive to the obedience of Christ." Do you hear the sense of conflict that comes through that passage? Paul clearly informs his readers that they are in a battle against unseen entities and that the battle is intense. He reminds the Corinthians to look beyond visible appearances and to use the spiritual weapons God has given them. These weapons are able to destroy everything raised up against the knowledge of God.

Paul's observation gives us great insight into where the majority of this battle occurs. Most of it is between our ears. Our minds, our belief systems, our worldviews—this is where the enemy aims. If we had any doubt that this is what Paul is thinking, we can find another penetrating insight earlier in 2 Corinthians: "The god of this world has blinded the minds of the unbelieving so that they might not see the light of the gospel of the glory of Christ, who is the image of God" (2 Cor. 4:4). In this verse and many others, the battle is for the spiritual comprehension that takes place in the mind.

Because salvation involves our minds and the way we see things, we tend to think that the knowledge of God is an intellectual issue. But it is more than that—it's a spiritual and moral issue. The god of this world has a master strategy to blind the minds of people so that they will not be able to grasp the truth. That's why intercessory prayer is so crucial—there's a vital relationship between acceptance of the gospel and the invisible war. Again, I don't know exactly how it works, and I won't even pretend that I can fully explain it, but the truth of this conflict flows right out of the New Testament text. There's a connection between people praying and the ability of those for whom they pray to see. When people are coming to Christ, I can guarantee you that somewhere, somehow, someone believes in prayer—and is actually doing it, not just talking about it.

Jesus knew the battle was real. When he was in agony in the Garden of Gethsemane the night before his crucifixion, he was tempted to quit. When life got hard, he never put on a superhero cape and forgot about being a man. He was fully God, but he was also fully man, and the Bible tells us he was tempted in every way like we are. That means he was tempted with lust, with anger, with depression, with envy, and with a false belief that people probably wouldn't accept his sacrifice, so why bother. He agonized to the point of sweating drops of blood.

What did Jesus do to overcome this battle? He prayed. His three closest friends were there with him, and the one thing he asked them to do was to pray. He had a need in his life, he was in the heat of spiritual conflict, and his greatest resource was prayer. Earlier that night he had told Peter that Satan had requested to sift him like wheat. "But I have prayed for you," Jesus said (Luke 22:31–32). We might wonder why Jesus, being God incarnate, didn't just speak a word and make the enemy go away. But we have to remember that one of the reasons he came was to model for us what it means to walk in complete dependence on the Father in the power of the Holy Spirit. So on the night when he was fighting his greatest battle, and Peter, one of his friends, was the target of the enemy's attack, Jesus demonstrated the solution for us. He prayed—a lot.

We'll discuss details of this kind of prayer later, but do you understand the implications? There is a visible and an invisible world that intersect, and we live in the intersection. A cosmic conflict is raging, and it has eternal implications. The souls of men and women, of little boys and girls, of people of every nationality and color and language all over the planet are at stake. The enemy seeks to blind us all to the truth, to dull our souls and ruin our lives. That's what spiritual warfare is all about.

As I began to prepare a series of messages on this subject a couple of years ago, a lady pulled out in front of me and totaled my car. I didn't think much of it at first. No one got hurt, so it wasn't that big a deal. Then two days later, we were having some bushes taken out of our yard, and one little sprinkler was broken. That wasn't a big deal either, except that the guy who came to fix the sprinkler cut the telephone line—the first time that had happened in twenty-six years of work, he said—and on top of that, our whole water system wouldn't work. My wife and daughter and I counted fifteen or sixteen crises in a matter of five days, to the point that it got laughable. All of a sudden I was up to my ears in things that I would have to deal with and that would distract me from preparing those messages.

Coincidence? I don't think so. This kind of thing happens much too often, and it's not just to me—this is a widespread testimony among many Christians. When I was a pastor in Santa Cruz, we would some-times have musicals during which we could often see hundreds of people come to Christ. I've had as many as three or four appliances go out in the twenty-four hours before these events. I understand the physics of it all, of course, but there's more to it than that. Annoying mishaps always seem to cluster around times of spiritual fruitfulness. That's not exactly coincidence.

I was preparing to teach on spiritual warfare for our staff at Walk Thru the Bible when I noticed something unusual. It began as a normal day—actually an exceptionally good one. I woke up early and had a great quiet time. My wife was especially gracious that morning and offered me some coffee in bed. It just doesn't get any better than that, does it? And then she came by a little bit later and offered me a second cup. What a great day! I had a meaningful time with the Lord and then went to work like I always do. But about an hour before I was to teach, it was as though a black curtain dropped over me. Nothing was wrong, as far as I could tell. My relationship with God was great, my wife was being loving and caring, and my family was fine. But all of a sudden I had thoughts like: "I don't want to live anymore." "I don't want to teach this." "I don't want to be the president of Walk Thru the Bible." "I'm a terrible person." It was instant, like walking in the sunshine one minute and wandering in the middle of the night the next. For half an hour, I was in a stupor. Being the superintelligent guy that I am, I had no clue why. I couldn't make the connection. Then a little voice inside my head said, "Hey, Chip, aren't you teaching on spiritual warfare? Hello. Did you ever think this might be a part of it?" So I prayed and confronted the enemy, and in moments I was walking out of the darkness and back into the light.

I know I'm not the only person to get suddenly depressed like that. Nearly everyone experiences discouragement, and a lot of times the reasons aren't very clear. There are many, many reasons for depression and discouragement—medical, chemical, psychological, social, and the like—but when dark moments strike out of the blue for no apparent reason, it should sound an alarm. One minute you're thinking about how well things are going and the next you're on a downward spiral of negative thoughts. Why? Because there are invisible realities that have everything to do with whether you experience the abundant life that Jesus promised, serve fruitfully in God's kingdom, and know the joy of your salvation.

**Personal Application: What about You?**

When was the last time you honestly considered that some struggle or relational conflict had its roots in satanic opposition? I know some people carry this concept too far, thinking that every flat tire comes from the flat-tire demon or every burned steak comes from the too-hot-barbecue demon. Or like the woman who showed up late for work, never did a very good job, and then blamed evil spirits when she got fired, many people use spiritual warfare as an excuse to avoid personal responsibility. But I'm not referring to the extremes here. I'm talking about regular, ordinary people who don't see a demon behind every bush, who love God, and who have normal conflict and struggles. Using good, biblical common sense, when was the last time some things happened to you that you really couldn't explain any other way? Like a relationship with someone you love and trust, for example, suddenly going south for no apparent reason? Or a church that God has really used suddenly boiling over in controversy, and no one can really put a finger on where it all began? Or a sense of oppression or depression that comes upon you in spite of the fact that your circumstances haven't taken a turn for the worse? When things are amiss, do you just chalk it up to chance or human nature? Or do you really consider whether there's a spiritual conflict going on behind the scenes?

Elisha saw the heavenly battle. An angel revealed a glimpse of it to Daniel. Paul wrote about it often. And Jesus, the incarnate God who knew all about the invisible world, encountered Satan and demons frequently. The early readers of biblical texts didn't think this was strange. They didn't regard the prophets and apostles as fringe wackos. They understood very well the truths that we need to get a firm grasp of today. The problems we face aren't really about our mates, our children, our jobs, or our circumstances. Behind all of those things is the subject of our basic truths numbers three and four: a malicious, personal archenemy who wants to use anything he can to destroy our lives.

## In Your Life

- What is your reaction to people who periodically attribute their problems to demonic activity?
- Are there times when you consider their explanations valid? Are there times when you dismiss them right away? What makes the difference?
- Can you identify any current difficulties in your life that may be the product of spiritual opposition?
- Have you seen any trends of opposition in your life—areas where God wants you to grow or serve and in which numerous obstacles come up?
- Have you been able to overcome these obstacles? Why or why not?

# 3

# You Have a Personal Enemy

> The existence of the devil is so clearly taught in the Bible that
> to doubt it is to doubt the Bible itself.
>
> Archibald Brown

It's Super Bowl Sunday, and both teams are ready. They have dreamed about this all season, but for the last two weeks they've done a lot more than dream. They have watched films. Hour after hour after hour they've sat in front of a screen, clicking the remote to speed the film forward, pressing it to rewind it back a few seconds, watching their opponent's plays over and over again. They've seen the other team's star quarterback pick apart defenses all season long, making mincemeat out of pass defenses. But they have reason to hope things will go better for their own defense.

What gives them more hope than the teams that were eliminated weeks ago? They know the opposition. They have learned the schemes. They know now that if the quarterback drops back three steps, he'll throw this pass 70 percent of the time and another pass 30 percent of the time. They know that if he rolls right, he's likely to look for his tight end coming left. They've watched him receive his signals from the sideline and relay them to his linemen and wide receivers. They have spent some of their time running drills, but they have spent more time on their homework. There will be no surprises because they've done the math. Why? *Because they want to win.* They want to win so badly that they'll spend inordinate amounts of time for half the year neglecting their families, all so they can wear a Super Bowl ring on their finger and tell viewers they're going to Disneyland. They take this stuff seriously because they'll lose if they don't.

## Basic Truth #3: Our Foe Is Formidable

Paul urges the Ephesians to take their battle more seriously than Super Bowl contenders, even more seriously than wartime troops. We saw in the last chapter just how much is at stake in this conflict. It has eternal consequences. And not only is the war intense, so is the enemy. Truth number three is an unpleasant but necessary subject of study: *our foe is formidable, and his goal is to destroy us and discredit the cause of Christ* (Eph. 6:12).

My friend Rick Dunham and I were studying Ephesians 6, and he summarized the enemy's goal like this: "Satan and his forces have a plan to terrorize your soul, to render you impotent as a believer, to make you worthless to the cause of Christ, and to make your life one of misery and spiritual defeat." Did you realize that? There are demonic spirits who want to terrorize you and make you miserable. I know that's a strong statement, but look at what Peter says about it: "Be of sober spirit, be on the alert. Your adversary, the devil, prowls around like a roaring lion, seeking someone to devour" (1 Peter 5:8). Scripture tells us to be watchful—to get on top of our game—because our enemy isn't playing tag. He's seeking someone to devour.

The lion is a powerful image. Lions prowl around for one reason: they are looking for something easy to kill. We usually don't fall victim to our enemy when we're strong. He is watching for us at the right time in the right way: when we're alone, tired, or traveling, or when it's late at night after everyone has gone to bed. Whenever we may be vulnerable, that's when something pops up on our computer screen and catches us off guard, or something comes on the TV that we would never watch with someone else in the room. Our initial reaction is shock and dismay, only we don't change the channel right away, and all of a sudden we're hooked. Or maybe we're hurting inside and some false belief system comes our way promising a deeper and more fulfilling experience—outside of Christ. There are many opportunities for the lion to find us vulnerable, and he knows how to spot them in our relationships, in our work, in our faith, in our spiritual disciplines—everywhere.

Not only does he try to devour us on the front end, he comes along afterward to smother us in guilt and condemnation. "You call yourself a Christian? Real Christians don't do what you just did. You're a terrible person, a hypocrite, not even close to the real deal." The initial temptation is powerful, but sometimes the shame of giving in to it is even worse. He plays us off of ourselves to put us into a downward cycle of failure and guilt.

Christians who take Satan lightly are ignoring biblical instructions. He is a formidable foe. We need to have a healthy respect for him. Jude 9 says that Michael the archangel, in a dispute with the devil, did not pronounce a railing judgment against him but simply said, "The Lord rebuke you!" We are not more formidable than Satan, but God is. Our proper attitude is to understand the capabilities of this angelic being and to depend on God's strength for victory.

## Is Satan for Real?

The Bible isn't ambiguous on the reality of Satan. He's there in the beginning in Genesis 3:1, tempting Eve. He's there in the middle in 1 Chronicles 21:1, inciting David to take a faithless census. He's there in the end in Revelation 12:9, hurled from heaven along with his fellow rebels to the earth. We've already explored many other passages that indicate his existence and his activity. I would encourage you to simply read through many of these passages, one right after the other. There's an enormous amount of biblical material on Satan and demons, leaving no doubt in Scripture that he's for real.

Jesus certainly thought Satan was real. He referred to Satan twenty-five times and had a personal encounter with him in Matthew 4:1–11. Someone has calculated that 25 percent of Jesus's actions, parables, and miracles had to do with demons. I don't know if that's an exact figure, but it's close. Jesus clearly thought demons were real. The letters and records of the early church in the New Testament were always written with the awareness of that context. Even Jesus's opponents knew Satan was "the prince of demons" (Luke 11:15 NIV). We'll examine his multiple titles in the coming pages, but the sheer number of them is a powerful testimony to the biblical assumption of his existence. This isn't a fringe topic in the far corners of Christianity.

In many modern cultures, Satan's existence is well known (and pretty easily seen). Western culture's reluctance to acknowledge his presence can be attributed to the fact that he has disguised himself well. Somehow he has convinced us that he's a cartoon character (a man dressed in a red suit and carrying a pitchfork), or a football mascot (Red Devils, Blue Devils, Sun Devils), or just a philosophical metaphor for evil (the dark side of "the Force" or the secret desires of human nature). Metaphors are hard to confront in prayer, so it is often in his best interest to deceive cultures into believing he's a figment of our imagination. As the senior devil in C. S. Lewis's *Screwtape Letters* instructs the junior devil, "Suggest to him a picture of something in red tights, and persuade him that since he cannot believe in that (it is an old textbook method of confusing them) he therefore cannot believe in you."[2] Satan is always content to hide in the shadows of a worldview if he can exploit that worldview to his own ends.

## Who Is Satan?

Who then is this formidable foe? According to Job 1:6 and Colossians 1:16, he's a created spirit. Matthew 25:41 and Revelation 12:7 refer to him and his minions as angels. A cherub is the kind or category of angel he is (Ezek. 28:14). That word *cherub* conjures up images of greeting cards on Valentine's Day, but cherubs in Hebrew Scripture are not cute, puffy little cupids. They are the highest class of angelic being, and Ezekiel 28 says Satan was the highest of them. So he was the highest angel of the highest class of angels—the greatest created being.

Are you starting to get a picture of how formidable our foe is? This is not a game; the battle is for keeps. In our flesh, we are no match for him. If we were to face him on our own, we would be overpowered and outsmarted in less than a second. The truth—which we will spend the rest of this book discussing—is that we are *not* left to face him on our own. That's the good news. But before we learn to rely on God's strength and wisdom, we need to come to terms with the insufficiency of our own.

## Where Did Satan Come From?

The two core Old Testament passages about Satan are Ezekiel 28 and Isaiah 14. Both of those passages point to dual realities, as much of Scripture does. Each speaks of a historical figure—the king of Tyre in Ezekiel and the king of Babylon in Isaiah—but those historical figures are windows into the true spiritual force behind them. Through these passages and other supporting verses, we can see that Satan (then Lucifer) was created perfect (Ezek. 28:12–13). He had a heavenly estate (Jude 6). His job was to be the guardian of God's glory (Ezek. 28:14). According to Ezekiel, he had more power than anyone in the universe except for God, and he was more beautiful than anything or anyone but God. Those attributes led to his fatal flaw. The occasion of his sin—his rebellion against God—was pride (Isa. 14:13; 1 Tim. 3:6).

That's not exactly consistent with our warped view of a guy dressed in a red suit and holding a pitchfork. The Satan of Scripture was the most intelligent, beautiful being in the universe that God created. His beauty and power led to prideful ambition. He got full of himself and wanted to be God. He made a conscious, purposeful choice—the kind of decision for which we are all responsible (Hab. 1:13; James 1:13). Satan's prideful rebellion is characterized by five "I will" statements in Isaiah 14:13–14:

- "I will ascend to heaven." He wanted to occupy the abode of God and have equal recognition with his Creator.
- "I will raise my throne above the stars of God." The stars in this context are the other angels. Satan wanted the greatest allegiance and respect from all creation.
- "I will sit on the mount of assembly." The mount of assembly is where God ruled. Satan wanted the highest position of authority.
- "I will ascend above the heights of the clouds." Clouds in Scripture usually indicate the glory of God. Satan wanted the glory due only to God. God's answer to that, of course, is that he does not share his glory with another.
- "I will make myself like the Most High." That has always been Satan's ultimate goal—to replace God and to receive all the beauty, glory, wisdom, and power of God.

When Scripture speaks of Satan, it isn't confined to small, passing comments or figures of speech. Satan is not a metaphor for evil. He is a powerful angel who committed treason against his Creator and convinced a third of the angels to rebel along with him. He now seeks to destroy all that is good and God-ordained, and his strategy ever since his fall has been to tempt us with the same agenda he had—to be like God.

We can see Satan's plan very early in Scripture. The first sin in the Garden of Eden was a product of that strategy. He told Eve that if she ate of the forbidden tree, she would be "like God" (Gen. 3:5), and that's how he continues to tempt us today. He knows so well how to tempt us with that desire because it is the desire that has filled his heart. He is intimately acquainted with prideful ambition.

The truth is that we can't be on equal terms with God. There is one Creator, and everyone else is a creature. We know that intellectually, and we don't consciously aspire to be God. But we *do* aspire to be the god of our own lives. While all of God's created beings are designed to know him, be loved by him, worship him, and have lives that are filled with fruitfulness and joy, the heart of sin is to cross that line between creature and Creator and say, "I want to be like God. I want to be the center of attention. I want life to be about my dreams, my agenda, and my fulfillment." The thinking of every human being has been corrupted in some degree by that spirit. It's the spirit of Satan and the essence of his temptations.

## Personal Application: What about You?

Sometimes when I teach this material, something happens in the expressions of the people in the audience. There comes a moment when people realize that this is real. It's serious. Life is not a game. Intellectually, a lot of Christians believe in Satan and demons, but that belief doesn't always sink in. When we start to process this information and see some potential areas where spiritual conflict is happening in our lives, we live with a deeper awareness and a greater sense of urgency. We understand the reason for Peter's instructions, and we begin to make decisions based on our new understanding. Awareness makes us sober and alert, always conscious that there is an adversary who is prowling around because he wants to destroy those who believe in God and blind those who don't.

## Basic Truth #4: We Must Respect Our Foe but Not Fear Him

Truth number four is essential to help us prepare for the battlefield: *we must respect our foe but not fear him; we must become acutely aware of his methods but not be preoccupied with them.* Even though Satan is more powerful than we can imagine and more deceptive than we can understand, we give him too much credit—or give God too little credit—if we fear him. We are to respect our enemy and never be casual about his threat, but we are not told in the Bible to be preoccupied with him. Our preoccupation should be entirely on God and not on our adversary or ourselves.

We do, however, need to be aware of the enemy's strategies. Like the defense preparing for the Super Bowl, we can prepare for demonic attacks with an understanding of what may be coming against us.

Paul encouraged the Corinthians to live with such awareness. There was a situation of immorality with a member of the fellowship, but the church had already exercised discipline, the man had already repented, and Paul had already forgiven him. The church, however, did not seem to be responding positively, perhaps holding a grudge toward the offender. Paul urged them to reaffirm their love rather than harbor bitterness. He emphasized that he forgave in order that "no advantage would be taken of us by Satan; for we are not ignorant of his schemes" (2 Cor. 2:11). Satanic schemes are designed to get a foothold in our lives, through unforgiveness or some other attitude not based in God's character or plan. Anger is another such attitude. Paul told the Ephesians that holding on to anger can give the devil an opportunity (Eph. 4:26–27). The goal of the enemy's schemes is to produce bitterness and hard hearts within the church, and we need always to be aware of what's going on.

Did you notice the nature of those schemes? We tend to think that demonic activity has to do with weird, paranormal phenomena—*The Exorcist* in real life. That assumption is dangerous because it allows us to ignore the invisible war. Creepy demonic manifestations are rare and bizarre, and most of us don't ever encounter those phenomena. When we read these passages about Satan's activity, however, it's clear that the issues are usually things like unwillingness to forgive, bitterness, anger, deceived minds, and any other attitude that can break a marriage, split a church, cause depression, turn people inward, and destroy our bodies with ulcers and anxieties. Those are not rare manifestations. They are the kinds of things we encounter every day. That makes our knowledge of the invisible war a necessary and practical understanding for getting through normal life situations. Paul made it clear that evil spirits have specific schemes and that we need to be intelligent and informed about them.

How can we make sure we are not ignorant of Satan's schemes? That is the vital question. Many of us just don't have a clue what Satan is doing or how he operates. But if the stakes of this invisible war are as high as the Bible tells us they are, we *have* to know. We cannot afford to be indifferent. In this case, ignorance is not bliss; it is devastating.

## Satan's Names Reveal His Tactics

A friend of mine from Santa Cruz is a first-generation Japanese American and a teacher at a university. He once told me about his grandfather's involvement in World War II. His grandfather had been taught from an early age, as were most Japanese children, that the emperor was God. During the war, it was better to die for the cause—for their god—than to go home as a coward. My friend lamented, "My grandfather was a sincere, good man who gave his life for what he thought was a worthy cause, and he truly believed the emperor was a deity." One of the first things the emperor admitted after Japan's surrender was that he was not divine. That deeply imbedded cultural belief was a deception that destroyed the lives of my friend's grandfather and many others. I don't mean that throughout history every cause of every war was a demonic deception, although we could probably discover some satanic egos, greed, and power trips behind a lot of them. But in the case of my friend's grandfather, a blatantly wrong belief system led many to sacrifice themselves for a cause based on a lie. In retrospect, it's not hard to see who was behind it.

It *is* hard to see those strategies, however, when we're in the midst of the conflict. It helps to know ahead of time how he tries to ruin us. A good starting point for understanding Satan's schemes is to examine his names:

- *Satan* means "adversary" (Job 1:6–7; 1 Thess. 2:18). He opposes God's agenda, he works against God's plan, he violates God's character, and he assaults God's people. He makes it a point to get in the way.
- *Devil* means "slanderer" (1 Peter 5:8). One of his schemes will be to say false things about people and ruin their reputations. He loves to stir up false witnesses and juicy gossip in order to discredit a servant of God.
- *Lucifer* means "son of the morning" or "shining one" (Isa. 14:12). This means he is not going to come to you transparently ugly and scary but will appear beautiful and winsome. You'll be attracted to his agenda because he'll dress it up and seduce you with it.
- *Beelzebub* means "lord of the flies" (Matt. 12:24). It was a pagan idol supposed to protect from swarms of flies. Jews understood it as "the god of filth," which is an apt description of Satan.
- *Belial* was the name of a false god (2 Cor. 6:15). Anything Satan can do to divert worship from God and direct it toward himself interests him.
- *The evil one* (1 John 5:19) in Greek is the word for absolute corruption. He will influence anything he can to corrupt it and make it as evil as possible. That is why one young child can kill another with a hammer blow to the skull, as in a news report I read recently. Or someone can put a bomb on his body to blow up himself and others. Or a company can knowingly pour poison into our water because it would cost quite a bit more to dispose of it in a safer manner. There's evil in the world, and it comes from a wicked, corrupting influence.
- *The tempter* (1 Thess. 3:5) will exploit our perfectly good desires and entice us to fulfill them with artificial means. That is why all good gifts from above—food, rest, sex, ambition, and work, for example—have distorted and twisted variations that are far from the will of God.
- *The prince of this world* (John 12:31) is a master of false systems. He crafts entire schools of thought that can suck us in and destroy us. He's working to create an image of what is attractive for young girls,

convincing them that if they don't look like a cover of *Seventeen* or *Cosmopolitan*, they're not worth very much. He has a system that has convinced guys that they need ripped abs and a chiseled physique to be cool, all so they'll become self-absorbed or take steroids and ruin their health. He's convinced millions that until they get a certain kind of watch to wear and a luxury car to drive to their beach house, they haven't really succeeded yet. He's behind false religions, false philosophies, false doctrine, false morality, and every system of thought that cannot lead anyone to God. He has infiltrated governments, economies, educational institutions, and anything that has influence in this world. The conclusion John came to is sobering: "The whole world lies in the power of the evil one" (1 John 5:19).

- *The accuser of the brethren* (Rev. 12:10) will condemn you. He points out your sins—the sins God has paid for in blood and forgiven—and reminds you of them constantly. "You're a terrible Christian, a bad dad, a no-good wife, a worthless human being," he'll whisper. If you ever hear that voice, it does not come from God.

You won't find this name in the Bible, but Satan is the original SweetTart™ distributor. Do you remember eating those candies when you were young? They are sweet on the outside and sour when you bite into them. The enemy will come with something that is good on the outside—like a legitimate, strong desire for food, sex, or achievement—and offer it to you in the wrong way at the wrong time. He'll get you to believe that his counterfeit pleasure is the only way to satisfy your emotional needs. He'll offer sex to you from a video screen or in a perverted way, moving you away from what is good, true, loving, and wonderful, and twisting it into something that is evil and destructive in the end. It will always look and taste attractive—that is, until you bite into it. But the problem is that the sour part may not come for weeks, months, or even years. You can spend decades enjoying the sugary coating of sin, only to find out too late that when the sweetness is gone, there's nothing left but a sour taste.

Satan comes to us in a multitude of ways. The serpent of Genesis 3 is crafty, the dragon of Revelation 12 will scare you to death, the angel of light in 2 Corinthians 11:14 will win you over, and the father of lies (John 8:44) is behind it all. He is more of a heavyweight than we give him credit for.

## Satan Attacks God's Program, the Church

Satan is a master counterfeiter. His attacks against the work that God does in this world are often indirect. He crafts attractive alternatives to the gospel and the church, many of them containing a lot of truth—but with just enough error to poison the whole system. If he can get non-Christians to sincerely believe in a seemingly noble cause—a false belief system or a charitable work—he can convince them that they don't need the gospel at all. If he can get Christians to mix some of his deceptions into their faith, he can fool us into living according to the world even while we are convinced we are living according to the gospel. The subtleties of his schemes produce a huge selection of counterfeits to the real thing.

The New Testament spells out some of these attacks for us. Colossians 2:8 informs us that Satan takes people captive through false philosophies. In 1 Corinthians 10:20, he is exposed as the mastermind behind false religions. He inspires many people within his domain to pose as ministers. These false servants then lead people astray as they mix and mingle with true servants of God (2 Cor. 11:14–15). Satan also is the source of false doctrine through the teachings of many antichrists (1 John 2:18). Jesus told a parable in Matthew 13:24–30 in which Satan makes counterfeit disciples and scatters them among the real ones. False morals may seem like the product only of human ignorance to us, but 2 Thessalonians 2:7–12 attributes them to the work of the deceiver. According to the Bible, the source of all falsehood, all misguided worldviews, all counterfeit religions and philosophies, and all teachers of any belief other than faith in the gospel of Jesus Christ are instigated, inspired, and influenced by the father of lies.

## Satan Attacks God's People

The examples in that last paragraph are mainly about vast, complex systems of thought, but Satan can get much more specific than that. He and his legions have intimate knowledge of the way our minds work and the weaknesses we human beings have. From that knowledge he has developed a variety of schemes for particular people and circumstances. His attacks can corrupt large institutions and individual lives. He has an impressive array of intrusions into our lives.

We saw in Daniel 10, for example, that Satan can direct governments; an invisible "prince" was operating behind the kingdom of Persia. We saw in 2 Corinthians 4:4 that he prevents people from coming to faith in Christ by deception; he blinds their minds. He wields the power of death (Heb. 2:14); he persecutes believers (Rev. 2:10); he hinders—or even prevents—our service to God (1 Thess. 2:18); he alienates people and provokes schisms (2 Cor. 2:10–11); he plants doubts in our minds (Gen. 3:1–5); and he shapes sects and cults (1 Tim. 4:1). And if we consider the wide variety of sins that Scripture tells us are provoked by our adversary, it's easy to get overwhelmed: anger, pride, worry, self-reliance, discouragement, worldliness, lying, and immorality are all his inspiration.

Read through the list in that last sentence again. Have you been thinking of these things as character flaws? Weaknesses? Psychological kinks that can be worked out through therapy alone? The dark side of human nature? If so, you only partly understand these sins. We live them out as character flaws and emotional shortcomings, but behind them all is a malicious personality who delights in these affronts to God. The first rebel gets great satisfaction in leading human beings—made in the image of God, of all things—to rebel along with him and violate our Creator's character and purpose. The many, many ways the image of God in us has been twisted and distorted beyond recognition fit perfectly into the agenda of our adversary, and he does everything he can to ensure that God's image is not restored to us in Christ.

Armed with all the information about Satan we've covered in this chapter, see if you can find his trademark false values, distorted agendas, self-directed pursuits, and subtle half-truths in the following description. One of the biggest lies we fall for today is rampant even in our churches. He has convinced us that life is a playground, that our primary goal is to be happy, and that God is the cosmic vending machine that can make it happen.

Because we so desperately want life to be a playground, we do whatever we can to make it one. We go through life as consumers, shopping for the best toys we can find to make us happy, scouting out the best vacation spots to keep us rested and refreshed, and filling up our free time with diversion after diversion. After all, if life is a playground, our number one goal ought to be to enjoy it.

Somewhere along the way, our Christian culture bought into the assumption that God's primary purpose for us is to have fun and be personally fulfilled. Hollywood and Madison Avenue have done a great job of cultivating our desires. They tell us what it takes to be happy, giving us example after example of the good life—a carefree, satisfied existence that we can all have if we'll only buy the right products and take care of ourselves. Pleasure is ours for the taking if we will only buy into the formula. And pleasure, we're told, is what fulfillment is all about.

There's a lot of truth in that, of course. God *does* offer us fulfillment. But it's a by-product of our relationship with God, not our number one goal (see Matt. 6:33). Fulfillment in itself is a "me-oriented" objective. We are never told in Scripture to make happiness the object of our pursuit; that's idolatry. We can seek joy and fulfillment and all the things God has planned for us, but we are to seek them by seeking God himself. God is not an enemy of happiness; he just doesn't give it to us in the ways we expect. It's in his time, in his way, and as part of his plan.

Here's how Satan has taken a generous helping of truth and mixed it with lies. He has convinced us to make a deal with God. It's an unspoken deal that we think God agreed to, but he didn't. We believe that if we read our Bibles, pray a lot, go to church faithfully, live reasonably moral lives, and serve wherever we can—in other words, if we push all the right buttons—God will respond with prosperity, peace, and lots of nice times. That's what it takes to be happy. If we make God happy by doing all the right things, God will make us happy by blessing us in every area of our lives. Our marriages will be great, our kids will turn out almost perfect, and our work will be fruitful. We may not do it consciously, but our expectations make God out to be a cosmic vending machine.

I was on a call-in radio program to answer questions about my book *Love, Sex, and Lasting Relationships.* I talked about God's design for relationships and how our purity is integral to his plan. A lot of people call that kind of radio show trying to figure out how they can get out of their marriage and still not violate God's standards. One woman who called said to me, "I know one thing for sure. God wants me to be happy. And I'm not happy with my husband. I know the Bible says God hates divorce, but I know he'll forgive me because he wants me to be happy. So I'm going to divorce my husband." At least she was honest, but she had bought into this lie of the happiness cult, and she's not alone. Roughly 50 percent of evangelicals have done exactly what she did.

If this is our mind-set, what happens when we pursue happiness according to what we believe God surely wants for us and then we struggle with conflict and pain? We feel that God didn't live up to his end of the bargain. When circumstances don't make sense, a relationship goes wrong, financial hardship strikes, or there's emotional or physical hurt, we put our hands on our hips and say, "Why, God? I can't figure out what you're doing. I did all the right things. Why isn't this working out?"

That's a great example of what Satan's lies do to us. His deceptions are aimed ultimately at making us question God, doubt his goodness, and conclude that he doesn't have our best interests at heart. That's what he did with Eve in the first sin, and he's been following the pattern ever since.

Here's the truth that God tells us. Life isn't turning out to be a playground for one very good reason: it was never a playground to begin with. This fallen world is a battleground, not a playground. The bullets are real and the bayonets are awfully sharp. There are demonic powers that are secretly seeking to destroy your life, your marriage, your friendships, your self-image, and your confidence. The master strategy is to undermine your fruitfulness and discredit the name of Jesus.

Imagine being a soldier in our day carrying a heavy pack in the heat of battle. You hold an M-16 as you ride shotgun through the city. You and six other guys are supposed to check out a building that might have some terrorist insurgents inside. This isn't a game; in fact, one of your buddies got blown up during just such a mission yesterday. Today, however, after nervously looking around every corner, you don't find anyone. The building is empty, so you pause for a brief respite and open your rations. What is your response going to be when you put the first bite into your mouth? "Oh my, the food is really lousy here. They didn't use nearly enough seasoning, the portions are a little smaller than I prefer, and they don't even think to serve it warm. We really should let someone know about this." Maybe that's not all you feel strongly about, so you move on to other issues. "This gun is just too heavy; I don't think I'll take it with me tomorrow. And why do we have to carry these packs? These gas masks and chemical suits are overkill, in my opinion. Who came up with that idea? And this electronic gear is just taking up space. I'm not sure we're ever going to need it. Maybe tomorrow we can lighten the load and bring some video games and CD players instead."

That comment could only come from someone who is under the delusion that he is on a playground. A soldier in a war zone doesn't have time to complain about the little things. He's got bigger issues than the taste of his food or the weight of his equipment, and he understands how vital his supplies are. Lives are at stake, including his own. His expectation is that he will have to fight and that he will need to prepare himself not only to survive but also to win. And by God's grace, he'll make it back home one day—the battles don't last forever. But in the meantime, there is a mission to finish and it's game-face time. Lack of preparation isn't an option.

It isn't an option for us either. God wants us to be fulfilled, but right now there's a battle going on. Now if you really believed that, how would it affect you when you went to work each day? How would your attitude toward your relationships change? Would you react any differently to stress and conflict? If your expectations about your life reflected the fact that you're on a battleground rather than a playground, wouldn't a lot of things change—like your perspective, your goals, and your strategies to make it through each day? I think your whole life might take on a different meaning. Respecting how formidable the foe is—highly deceptive, very subtle, and always mixing a lot of truth with just enough lies to get us really mixed up—will help us see life from a much more accurate angle.

## Satan's Power Is Limited

If all of these biblical references about the awesome power of Satan are unnerving, remember the principle of basic truth number four: we do not need to fear our adversary. Yes, he has alarming capabilities, but God has greater capabilities, and he is on our side. While the Bible tells us often and emphatically that this war is real and the foe is to be respected, it never tells us to fear him. In fact, it gives us quite a few reasons to be confident.

First, it helps to remember that Satan is a created being. He is not God's counterpart. Some religions have a dualistic view of supernatural power; there is a battle between good and evil, and we hope good wins out. But that's not biblical—not at all. Scripture is very clear that God is omniscient, omnipotent, and infinite. Satan is none of these things. He knows a lot, but not everything. He has power, but not nearly as much as God. And his capabilities are not limitless. There are things he cannot do and places he cannot go.

Second, it is comforting to remind ourselves that Satan can be resisted by the Christian who relies on God. James 4:7 tells us to submit to God and resist the devil. If we do that, Satan will flee from us. He has to. He cannot compete with God in the life of a submitted Christian—or anywhere, for that matter. The enemy cannot remain where God exercises his power, and God exercises his power in us as we follow him. That's why the Bible never tells us to flee from Satan. If we trust God's truth, he has to flee from us instead.

Third, we need to remember that God places limitations on Satan. He wanted to wreak havoc in Job's life (Job 1:12), and God let him—but only to a point. God designated specific areas where the adversary was permitted to attack and specific areas where he was not. In other words, he is on a leash that is firmly held by the hand of our Father. He cannot do to us what God does not allow him to do.

## Personal Application: What about You?

It is crucial to be balanced and wise in our understanding of spiritual opposition. To assign too much or too little credit to the reality of demonic activity is to fall into great error. We need to understand what power Satan does and does not have. A Christian life that cannot walk the line between respecting the enemy while being preoccupied with God is a life that is out of balance. Our responsibility is to learn Satan's schemes and protect ourselves according to God's provision, but fear is an unbiblical and inappropriate response. Scripture does not tell us about the enemy in order for us to live anxious lives; we are told so we can prepare ourselves to win great victories. In order to do that, we next need to become grounded in the amazing truth that "greater is He who is in you than he who is in the world" (1 John 4:4). Basic truth number five will be the key to our confidence in the invisible war.

## In Your Life

- In which areas of your life do you suspect that you may have bought into Satan's deceptions? Does your work, your marriage, your plans for the future, or any other aspect of your life reflect any part of the adversary's agenda?
- Where do you see Satan's influence in the culture in which you live?
- In what ways can you as an individual stand firm against wide-spread, system-level influences?
- Do you have a greater tendency to assign too much or too little credit to the enemy? What steps do you need to take to achieve balance in your thinking?

# 4

# Our Strategic Position

The devil fears a soul united to God as he does God himself.

John of the Cross

We arrived in India six days after the tsunami hit. We had traveled over thirty hours straight, and I had hardly slept in the last three days. I would be teaching a citywide crusade in a city where 160 people were swept off the beach and a fishing village was destroyed.

The cab driver who took us into that city from the airport began to give us the lay of the land. "The people here are very mad at God," he told us. "They do not know why he is punishing them." He then described the spiritual climate as it related to Hindus, Muslims, and Christians. He painted a picture of doubt, desperation, and confusion. The church was in grave need, and yet it had an unprecedented opportunity to reach out to many who felt abandoned and betrayed by the gods they worshipped.

I fell asleep quickly that night but awakened within a couple of hours. My room was dark, my body was worn out, I was apprehensive about what I would teach the following day, and I was very vulnerable to spiritual attack. The following six hours would be among the worst of my life. It was as though I was under an all-out assault from hell itself. Thoughts of condemnation and death bombarded my mind for hours. The enemy whispered lie after lie into the recesses of my mind as I quoted Scripture and attempted to pray. Doubts that had not entered my mind since I was a new Christian came at me full force throughout the night. I felt lonely, weak, and completely inadequate for the task.

In desperation, I turned on my CD player, put on my headphones, and began to worship the Lord. I couldn't pray, I couldn't think, and I couldn't concentrate. After hours of battle and feeling very defeated, I couldn't address the enemy anymore. All I could think was that God inhabits the praises of his people (Ps. 22:3). At first I felt nothing. But little by little, as I sang in adoration, the grip of darkness in the room was broken.

I met my friend and colaborer, Phil, for breakfast and shared my exhausting experience with him. He immediately asked me what time it began because he had gone through a similar experience. He had found relief only by reading through 1 and 2 Peter multiple times during the night.

As we approached the ministry in India together, the needs seemed so overwhelming—and we felt so weak and inadequate—that we questioned what real good we could do in the situation. We were two senior leaders of an international Christian ministry with the awesome opportunity to give people hope for both now and eternity, and yet we were struggling. We were vulnerable to the enemy's shots of doubt, condemnation, and deception coming our way.

We both experienced a major breakthrough and saw God do amazing things at the crusade. We had an overflow crowd of thousands at our all-day seminar on "The Miracle of Life Change" from Ephesians 4. We saw Christians rise up in faith and give generously to relieve the needs of both Christians and non-Christians in the city. God was triumphant, and we were delivered.

How? The key came through a phone conversation Phil remembered having with his son six months earlier when we were in east Asia. We were hours ahead of U.S. time zones, and the Olympics were being taped and rebroadcast back home. Phil's son was less than attentive to his father's phone call, explaining that the U.S. basketball team was on TV and losing by ten points. Phil encouraged him by assuring him the United States would win. What his son didn't know was that the game was already over, and we knew the final score.

"No, Dad, you don't understand," Phil's son told him. "We're losing and it doesn't look good at all." Phil nevertheless guaranteed that despite how things looked, our basketball team would win. "You can relax; this is going to come out just fine."

Maybe it sounds strange, but God used that random conversation to restore my perspective. Phil and I had battled through some of the most severe opposition we had ever faced, and in the midst of it, I had forgotten one of the most important aspects of spiritual warfare: we do not fight *for* victory but *from* victory. Just as Phil knew the final outcome of the basketball game while his son agonized over it, we know the final

We fight from victory, not for victory.

outcome of our battles in spite of their fierceness. Somehow, in the wee hours of the morning as I was fighting doubts and condemnation, I lost sight of the airtight reality that the victory has already been won by Jesus. Spiritual warfare is never an attempt to gain the victory. It is standing firm in what we already possess.

## Basic Truth #5: We Do Not Fight *for* Victory; We Fight *from* Victory

There's an extremely important fact that every believer must clearly understand before any engagement in this battle. If, in your mind, this fact is still up in the air, you will not be able to experience very much victory in your life. It doesn't mean you won't have victory—the ultimate victory has already been won for you by Jesus. It does mean, however, that you will feel confused and defeated in trying to live the Christian life if you don't get this down, and you will miss opportunities to serve God and enjoy his blessings. The crucial fact that you need to know is basic truth number five: *As believers in Christ, we do not fight* for *victory; we fight* from *victory. In Christ's power, we are invincible.*

I'm not trying to be clever with semantics here. There's a huge difference between fighting *for* victory and fighting *from* victory. I've emphasized that there is an invisible world, an invisible war, and a formidable foe, and that we need to respect but not fear that foe. The reason we don't need to fear him is because of the wonderful fact that Jesus has already won this battle. We'll explore why the battle still rages in the next chapter, but until we get there, we need to understand that the outcome is certain. There's no suspense in the kingdom of God about how it will turn out.

That means that when we fight, we're not trying to win. We're enforcing the victory that Jesus has already secured. In his power, we are invincible.

We know the victory is won before we ever even put on the armor, not only from what the rest of the New Testament tells us but more specifically because of where Paul's instructions come in the letter to the Ephesians. When Paul began this letter, he wrote of what Christ had accomplished. The first three chapters tell of the amazing transformation that comes through the grace of God. We've been transferred from the kingdom of darkness to the kingdom of light, the kingdom of God's beloved Son. We've been rescued from death to life, redeemed, made brand new, given an eternal inheritance, and sealed in the Spirit. Now we've been brought into a new entity called the church—a mystery hidden in the heart of God from eternity past. This mystery brings Jew and

Gentile, slave and free, and male and female into one new relationship and one new body.

When chapter 4 of Ephesians opens, Paul tells us about the supernatural life we now have with God the Father through our relationship with Christ. The Holy Spirit dwells within us, and we are to walk in a manner worthy of our calling—in purity and light. Chapter 5 explains what being children of light means for husbands and wives, and chapter 6 applies it to parents and children and masters and servants. Only then, after all of the glorious commentary on the new life, does Paul warn his readers that this life will be lived out in a hostile environment (Eph. 6:10–20). We live in a fallen world, and though we are brand new, we still fight a war on two fronts. Our flesh wages war against the Spirit—that's one front—and we battle against a supernatural, angelic being who fell from heaven, who took a third of the angels with him, and whose goal is to destroy us spiritually, emotionally, relationally, and physically—that's the second front. Fighting on both fronts will require all of our resources. The good news is that Jesus *is* our resource.

It is comforting that Paul describes this battle after he has already written emphatically about Jesus's victory and our new life. He didn't give instructions about our warfare and then follow it up with a discussion of victory. He began with the victory and ended with the warfare. The order is reassuring, especially for those who are waiting to win their battles before they can enjoy the Christian life. This entire Ephesian letter promises us that the triumph is already accomplished.

I don't know what your past experience with Scripture memory is, but even if you have never memorized a single verse, the following four verses should be the next ones you memorize. These promises will remind you of who you are and what you have. Whenever you are feeling defeated, discouraged, and anything but invincible in your battles, rehearse these promises often. They have the potential to change the direction of your prayer life and align you with the truth God has given. Your feelings will not always reflect God's truth accurately; the facts presented in these verses will. Let them sink in and transform your thinking so you can know the position from which you fight.

1 John 4:4—"You are from God, little children, and have overcome them; because greater is He who is in you than he who is in the world." That's a fact. God's Spirit dwells within you, and Satan is the prince of this world. That means that whenever you and this world clash, or whenever you and the evil spirits influencing this world clash, you have the upper hand. The Spirit within you has already overcome them.

1 John 5:4–5—"Whatever is born of God overcomes the world; and this is the victory that has overcome the world—our faith. Who is the one who overcomes the world, but he who believes that Jesus is the Son of God?" If you are born of God, there is no reason not to overcome. If you are a child of God, you have the victory.

Revelation 12:11—"They overcame him because of the blood of the Lamb and because of the word of their testimony, and that they did not love their life even when faced with death." The saints relied on the victory of Jesus—the blood of the Lamb—and their testimony of his triumph. They stood firm against the enemy, even when it cost them their lives.

James 4:7—"Submit therefore to God. Resist the devil and he will flee from you." This dual approach of submitting to God and resisting the devil is an invincible stance. God's promise is certain. Those who, in obedience to God, are living for him and resisting the enemy will overcome.

## Personal Application: What about You?

Before we go any further, let this sink in. Satan is a defeated foe. Jesus said he came to destroy the works of the devil, and in John 12:31 he asserted that the time had come for the ruler of this world to be cast out. Whenever we are in the heat of battle, we are not subject to defeat if we rely on Jesus's victory and the promises of God. If we know how to put on our armor and to stand firm, and if we know how to pray according to Paul's instructions in Ephesians 6, the triumph of Jesus is our triumph too. In the next section, we'll explore more deeply how to prepare ourselves for the fight and discover the invincible equipment we've been given. But as we prepare, we must always be armed with the right mentality. Jesus has won. We fight from victory.

## In Your Life

- Do you struggle with a sense of defeat? In what ways can basic truth number five help you?
- How does your understanding of your position in Christ affect the way you pray?
- What is the value of memorizing the four verses in this chapter?
- What truth from Spiritual Warfare 101 has been most helpful to you? Why?

## What You Need to Remember

1. *Satan is a defeated foe.* Jesus assured his disciples of that, and he gave us plenty of examples of his authority to proclaim judgment on the evil one. "Now judgment is upon this world; now the ruler of this world will be cast out" (John 12:31).
2. *Jesus destroyed the works of the devil.* Satan comes to steal, kill, and destroy. Jesus came that we might have abundant life (John 10:10). "When He had disarmed the rulers and authorities, He made a public display of them, having triumphed over them through Him" (Col. 2:15).
3. *We are victors in Christ.* The crucifixion, resurrection, and ascension of Jesus have won for us everything we need in this battle—even overcoming death. "'O death, where is your victory? O death, where is your sting?' The sting of death is sin, and the power of sin is the law; but thanks be to God, who gives us the victory through our Lord Jesus Christ" (1 Cor. 15:55–57).
4. *We have the power and resources to resist Satan and demonic attacks.* That power and those resources dwell within us in the Spirit of God. "Greater is He who is in you than he who is in the world" (1 John 4:4).
5. *We must learn how to put on the full armor of God to experience in daily living the victory we already possess.* "Take up the full armor of God, so that you will be able to resist in the evil day, and having done everything, to stand firm. Stand firm therefore, having girded your loins with truth, and having put on the breastplate of righteousness, and having shod your feet with the preparation of the gospel of peace; in addition to all, taking up the shield of faith with which you will be able to extinguish all the flaming arrows of the evil one" (Eph. 6:13–16).

# Spiritual Warfare 201

## How to Prepare Yourself for Spiritual Battle

You were rubbed with oil like an athlete—Christ's athlete—as though in preparation for an earthly wrestling match, and you agreed to take on your opponent.

Ambrose of Milan

Therefore, take up the full armor of God, so that you will be able to resist in the evil day, and having done everything, to stand firm. Stand firm therefore, having girded your loins with truth, and having put on the breastplate of righteousness, and having shod your feet with the preparation of the gospel of peace.

Ephesians 6:13–15

## Introduction: Basic Training

After the treaty that ended World War II was signed, pockets of guerrilla warriors continued to fight on hundreds of islands throughout the Pacific. The bullets were just as real, and the casualties were just as dead. In the same way, Satan continues to fight even after Jesus has won the victory.

1. Satan was *defeated* at the cross.
2. Sin's *penalty* was paid for all people for all time.
3. Sin's *power* was broken.
4. Yet Satan and his host of fallen angels continue to engage in guerrilla warfare to discourage, deceive, divide, and destroy God's people and God's program.
5. Believers are commanded to *equip* and *prepare* themselves in the strength of the Lord and in his mighty power to stand firm against the enemy's schemes, repel his multifaceted attacks, and engage and defeat him in specific battles.

# Executive Summary

## Review

The question: how does this work?

The answer: four keys to spiritual victory.

    a. We must become aware of the invisible war (section 1).

    b. We must learn to appropriate God's protection for daily living (section 2).

    c. We must learn to engage the enemy with supernatural weapons (section 3).

    d. We must utilize God's means of deliverance when spiritually attacked (section 4).

1. How can you prepare yourself for satanic attack?
   a. Ephesians 6:13—Our Commander (Jesus Christ) *urgently* commands us to pick up our spiritual armor and put it on. Why? For the purpose of being *fully prepared* and *enabled* to withstand the dark times when the enemy attacks.
   b. Ephesians 6:14a—After picking up our armor in preparation for battle, we are then commanded to *consciously* and *vigorously* make a *decisive act* (or succession of acts) to stand our ground firmly and fearlessly against the enemy's assaults as he seeks to deceive, accuse, and discourage us.
   c. Ephesians 6:14b–15—Using the metaphor of a Roman soldier's armor (which protected him in battle), we are given three specific pieces of spiritual armor that must be put on by believers as a *prerequisite* to standing firmly and fearlessly against demonic attack.

2. "Having girded your loins with truth."
   a. The metaphor explained: The belt was critical to the rest of the equipment. All of the armor connected to it.
   b. "Truth": candor, sincerity, truthfulness rooted in the objective reality of the truth of God's Word, but here it refers to the subjective, practical application of openness and honesty in all things with God and man.
   c. Satan's first attack on humankind was *deception*, which was followed by our hiding, denial, and blame-shifting.

d. The belt of truth is evident in the man or woman whose mind "will practice no deceit and attempt no disguises in their walk with God."[3]

e. Application: Psalm 139:23–24. "Search me, O God, and know my heart; try me and know my anxious thoughts; and see if there be any hurtful way in me, and lead me in the everlasting way."

3. "Having put on the breastplate of righteousness."

a. The metaphor explained: The breastplate covered more than the midsection, from the neck to the thighs. It was also called a "heart protector."

b. "Righteousness": uprightness, right living, integrity in one's lifestyle and character; conforming our will with God's will. Although rooted in the objective righteousness that we already possess in our standing before God through the work of Christ, this breastplate of righteousness (that guards and protects the heart) is the *practical application* of the truth to our lives. In other words, it's the lordship of Christ.

c. Satan's attacks are not merely deception but accusation of the believer, resulting in guilt and condemnation. When we willfully turn away from what we know is God's will, we open ourselves to demonic influence in our lives. (Old Testament example: Saul; New Testament example: Peter.)

d. Application: James 4:17. "Therefore, to one who knows the right thing to do and does not do it, to him it is sin." Personal area to address: Pray more intentionally.

4. "Having shod your feet with the preparation of the gospel of peace."

a. The metaphor explained: Roman sandals were tightly strapped to the entire lower leg and had nails protruding from them. They planted a soldier's feet in certainty.

b. "Preparation": establishment—the means of a firm foundation; also conveys the idea of readiness to share the gospel, which brings peace between people and God.

c. Satan not only uses *deception* and *condemnation* to neutralize believers, but he also specializes in *casting doubt* on the very basis of God's goodness and the means by which we have received it—the gospel. Satan attacks grace. How? 2 Corinthians 11:3–4.

*KEY*

d. Application:
* • *Know* and *understand* the content of the gospel (1 Cor. 15:1–6; Eph. 2:1–9).
  * Know the basis for your *eternal security* and the *assurance of your salvation* (security—Rom. 8:38–39; Eph. 1:13–14; assurance—1 John 5:11–13).
  * Faith is based on *facts*, not feelings.
  * Sharing your faith is one of the most powerful faith-builders available. Often "the best defense is a good offense."

*Preparedness*
*Alertness*

*Foundation*

God has objectively defeated Satan and his agenda. He has delivered us from sin's penalty and power, and ultimately he will deliver us from sin's very presence. In the interim, we are involved in guerrilla warfare with demonic forces.

As believers, we have been transferred from the kingdom of darkness to the kingdom of light, with all the rights, privileges, and position that being a child of God entails. The spiritual battle we fight involves a responsibility on our part to put on the spiritual protection that God has provided for us. We can and will resist the enemy's attempts to deceive, accuse, and cast doubt when we stand firm against him by:

1. being honest with God, ourselves, and others as a prerequisite to all spiritual battle,
2. responding to the truth that God shows us about his will for our lives—righteous living,
3. clearly understanding the gospel and habitually sharing this message of grace.

The great majority of spiritual warfare need never go beyond the regular practice of living out our position in Christ by faith. Our practice of Paul's metaphor of the spiritual armor protects us from Satan's ongoing attempts to break our fellowship with Jesus and, as a result, greatly minimizes any impact by the enemy.

There are times, however, when we must move beyond "standing firm" and engage the enemy in actual combat. This will be the topic of section 3 (Eph. 6:16–17).

Con

# 5

# Your Personal "Code Red"

Théoden: I will not risk open war.
Aragorn: Open war is upon you, whether you would risk it
or not.

from J. R. R. Tolkien, *Lord of the Rings*

My father was in the South Pacific when World War II ended, and he used to tell me about a very unusual period at the end of the war. The bombs had been dropped, the Japanese had surrendered, a treaty was signed, and the Pacific was at peace. Well, on paper it was at peace. My father said that on islands scattered throughout the region, battles raged. Though the outcome had already been determined, isolated Japanese units hadn't heard of the surrender. They continued to wage guerrilla warfare just as they had been doing during the war. The bullets were just as real, the people hiding in tunnels were still committed to killing their foes, the mortars were just as devastating, and death was just as brutal. Young men lost their lives to an enemy who had already surrendered. There was nothing at stake between the two countries anymore; the outcome was final. But the fighting wasn't over. And it was just as deadly as it had always been.

That's a picture that captures exactly where we are in the invisible war. The victory is already accomplished; absolutely nothing is at stake in terms of the ultimate outcome of Satan's rebellion against God. What continues to be at stake, however, is the lives of those who are still fighting. The enemy knows the war is already officially over, but he wants to wreak as much havoc as possible while he still can. Demonic spirits are still intent on destroying the people of God, and their weapons are as real as they always have been. So are the casualties. Though the victory is won, it has not yet been completely enforced.

Satan was defeated at the cross. Nothing can diminish that. His defeat was irrevocably sealed when Jesus conquered sin and death by dying and rising again. The penalty we incurred for our sin was paid, and its power was broken. Through the cross, Jesus disarmed and triumphed over the enemy. We've been taken from the kingdom of darkness and reborn into the kingdom of light. We have been given a new beginning; the old things are past, and all things are new. We've even been highly positioned, seated with Jesus in heavenly places. Yet we are still in a war.

Why? Just as peace had to be enforced in the Pacific, Jesus's victory must be enforced in our world. One day he will come again and do that finally and completely, and evil will be completely done away with. Meanwhile, there is guerrilla fighting all around us, and the strategy of the guerrillas is to deceive, discourage, divide, and destroy God's people and God's program. They employ terrorist tactics, and our alert signals should always be on "code red."

God says he wants to equip us and prepare us to walk in his strength so we can withstand the enemy's schemes and repel his multifaceted attacks. When we follow God's instructions, given through Paul in his letter to the Ephesians and through the rest of Scripture, we will be able to defeat Satan in the specific battles in our lives—at work, in our families, at church, and anywhere else the enemy is active.

How does that play out in our lives? We went a long way toward answering that question in the first four chapters—becoming aware of the invisible war is the first step in winning it. If Spiritual Warfare 101 helped you see beyond the external circumstances in your life to the spiritual influences that might be behind them, you've been properly enlisted and are ready for training. That's a major step in your preparation for conflict. You can't win a battle if you don't know you're in it.

There are four keys to spiritual victory (which is why this book is divided into four sections), and being aware of the battle was step one. Step two is basic training: appropriating God's ongoing protection for daily living. In this and the next three chapters, Spiritual Warfare 201, we'll look at the ways we can defend ourselves and obey the command to stand firm. God has given us armor; it's up to us to learn how to put it on and use it. Engaging the enemy and discovering God's means of deliverance will come later in Spiritual Warfare 301 and 401, but we don't want to charge into battle without any defensive armor. If we don't know how to protect ourselves, we'll end up wounded very quickly.

## How Can You Prepare Yourself for Satanic Attack?

Paul tells the Ephesians in 6:13–15 to take up the full armor of God so that they will be able to resist in the evil day. They are to do everything to stand firm. How? First, there are some basic pieces of equipment to put on—critical steps that every believer needs to take in order to withstand attacks. To communicate the principles of preparation, Paul uses the powerful word picture of a Roman soldier and his armor.

Before we go any further in this passage, remember that this armor is just a metaphor. Some commentators will argue that Paul was thinking of a passage in Isaiah in which God puts on a breastplate of righteousness and a helmet of salvation (Isa. 59:17). Other commentators will argue that this Roman soldier is strangely missing some standard equipment, such as a spear and other accessories. If you are looking for precision, please just relax and envision the metaphor. It's a picture—a familiar picture to Paul's readers—to help us understand the general thinking of how we can guard our lives and prepare ourselves for battle.

It's also important to remember that the armor is a description of how we are to live out a dynamic relationship with Jesus. This is a lifestyle, not a checklist. These pieces of protection aren't things that we can mechanically pray onto ourselves each morning in a step-by-step routine. It is a visual aid to help us understand how to live out a relationship with the Father in the power of the Holy Spirit. It is, of course, important to understand what these things are and apply them, but there's nothing ritualistic about them. Putting them on doesn't happen merely through a brief morning prayer time. It's a lifestyle issue—the product of weeks, months, and years of practice and cultivation. This is something we do, not a formula we recite.

Think of Paul's instructions in Ephesians, then, not as an equipment checklist but as a training manual in the proper usage of divine safeguards. This passage has all the elements of a drill sergeant of today calling the troops to assembly. If this were a modern scene, the sergeant would put his troops in rows and point to the equipment in front of each one of them. He would want them to know the ins and outs of their M-16s, the contents of their backpacks, the proper use of gas masks and of the special vial each one carries in case of chemical attack—every last instruction they might need before marching into the intensity of the battle. He would want it to be second nature to them so they would instinctively fall back on the appropriate tactics as the conflict raged. But Paul lived in a different day, and the picture he uses comes from the most powerful fighting force of his time. Roman armor conveys a sense of power, domination, prestige, and military efficiency. This kind of soldier represents the empire's authority.

There is no way to interpret this key passage on spiritual warfare casually. Jesus is our Commander-in-chief—the highest authority we will ever have—and through Paul, he charges his troops with a sense of urgency. The tense of the Greek verb used in the command to "take up the full armor of God" indicates something that must be done right now, immediately, as soon as possible. This is a top priority.

Why is this command such a high priority? Because an evil day is coming. That's not a prophecy, just a fact. When Paul tells his readers to take up their full armor so that they will be able to resist in the evil day, he is preparing them for the difficult times he knows are coming. He knows they will need to be fully prepared and enabled to withstand grave, dark times.

This term, *the evil day*, is an interesting phrase; it means "on a particular day at a particular time." Why? Because the battles aren't all the same. This conflict isn't about a constant, invisible source that keeps coming at you consistently every day. There are specific opportunities when the enemy will try to deceive you, discourage you, or turn you away from your Commander-in-chief, the Lord Jesus. We've discussed earlier how the lion prowls around for vulnerable prey. There are times when you are on the top of your game, so the enemy waits. He watches your seasons and cycles, looking for the times when you are weak. When you are tired, when you've had a conflict with your spouse, when the economy drops and you suddenly see how much security you had placed in your retirement plan, when you're in the ICU with one of your children and you wonder if he or she is going to make it—at any given moment of weakness, you can be tempted to think that God is not good.

Think about your experiences in prayer, for example. At some point in your life you have probably prayed and prayed for something that your heart desired deeply. As time passed, you may have wondered why God didn't seem very responsive to you. But you waited because that's what faith does. Then all of a sudden circumstances turned in the exact opposite direction from what you wanted. Not only did God not seem to be answering you positively, his will appeared to be contrary to yours. At just that time, you probably heard what every believer hears from time to time: a whisper that casts doubt on the goodness of God.

You know that little voice, don't you? When circumstances don't go your way, the whisper says, "See? God doesn't hear your prayers. Why do you give your life to a God who isn't listening?" If you're a single person who is not going out and having "a good time" like most of your friends, and God's provision for companionship still is not coming as quickly as you would like, you may suddenly start wondering whether it's worth it to live a pure life. That voice will call you a fool and constantly remind you of all the fun you're missing. Or perhaps you prayed for guidance before you took a certain job and were sure you had received it. Six months later, when you find out that the job doesn't fit your skills, that it is draining you of time and energy, and that the benefits don't live up to what you were promised, the whisperer will say, "God has hung you out to dry. You asked him for help, and he led you astray. It's better just to do what you want than to pretend like you're understanding his will." Why? Because that's what the lion does. He waits for your weakest moments. There's an evil day.

That's why this passage is written in such an urgent tone. We need to be prepared not just to resist when we are strong, confident, and on guard but also to resist when we are least able to do it. There are no times in our lives as Christians when we can sit back and relax, confident that we are out of view of the enemy. He comes with different tactics at different times because he wants to catch us off guard. Just as a quarterback doesn't call the same play on every down, or just as a con artist doesn't try the same scam twice on the same person, Satan will vary his strategies against you and do everything he can to surprise you. He knows you will probably be prepared where you failed last time, so he will come at you from different angles. His timing is what defines for you what "the evil day" is. And your readiness is an urgent matter.

In my life, that evil day often comes after some of my most fruitful work for God. After I have prepared thoroughly, gotten "prayed up," preached with a sense of God's presence, watched God work in a powerful way, and then counseled numerous people afterward as they share how God used his Word in their lives, I often struggle with waves of depression, condemnation, and bizarre thoughts of temptation that come from out of the blue. I am very vulnerable during those times—especially if I'm traveling—so I've learned to place extra safeguards around me then. Take a minute to ask yourself when and where you are most vulnerable. You'll be surprised how becoming aware of and preparing for that evil day can help you win a lot more of those battles.

After picking up our armor in preparation for battle, we are then commanded to consciously and vigorously make a decisive act (or succession of acts) to stand our ground firmly and fearlessly against the enemy's assaults (Eph. 6:14). We may not know exactly how he will attack in the evil day, but we know what his goals are: to deceive, accuse, and discourage us.

Notice that our stance is not offensive at this point. We are standing on ground that we already have. Imagine, for example, an army that has taken a town. One of the first things it does is secure the strategic areas so that the enemy can't retake the territory that has just been seized. It costs a lot in terms of strategy and lives to gain ground; no one wants to give up what he or she has gained. That's the picture in Ephesians. We must not give up what we have already gained through our relationship with Jesus.

If you're wondering what you have already gained, go back and read the first three chapters of Ephesians. We have been given a generous territory. We have come into the kingdom of light not only as full-fledged citizens but also as children of the King. Reading Ephesians thoroughly will give you a sense of just how extravagant God has been with us. We have his Spirit and his various gifts, we have been joined to the spiritual body of Christ, and we have been promised an inheritance that includes forgiveness, peace, and spiritual fruit. All of this is territory accomplished by Jesus and given to us by grace. When we prayed to receive Christ in faith, we received all of this as our possession.

As we walk in a manner worthy of our calling, as chapters 4 and 5 of Ephesians tell us to do, that evil, whispering voice—or the circumstances that Satan exploits—will try to encroach on our territory and make our walk in the light very difficult. Surely you've heard it: "You don't really have peace, do you?" "God loves the world in general, but not you individually." "Why forgive people who wouldn't do the same for you?" Step-by-step, the enemy will trespass on your life until the way you live and think are not much different from the way you used to live and think. He chips away until the new creature in you is obscured by your tendency to default to the old creature you once were.

So we are told to stand firm in the territory we have been given. It isn't that someone is just trying to knock us down. Someone is trying to steal the inheritance we have been given—or at least the experiential benefits of that inheritance. When we stand firm, we are holding on to our position, the area we already possess.

In order to hold our position, we need to be able to oppose and resist the enemy in the evil day—in other words, to stand firm. The grammar of the command here implies conscious and vigorous behavior in order to anchor ourselves on the possession God has won for us and to fearlessly withstand the enemy's assaults. His deceptions, accusations, and devious attempts to discourage can be firmly opposed if we understand the equipment we have been given. We must learn how to guard the territory that has been entrusted to us and not let our new position in Christ get undermined by our thinking, speech, and lifestyle. If you're wondering how this works out in everyday life with normal people like you and me, keep reading. We're just about to get there.

## Personal Application: What about You?

A "code red" has been issued for your life; there is no opting out. Some people think they can avoid the battle if they just ignore it, but the battle comes anyway. There are only two responses: do nothing or prepare. But the fact of the battle is a given.

Are you prepared? Are you guarding the territory entrusted to you with all the resources God has provided? There is a divine strategy and an array of supernatural armor and weapons at your disposal. When the opposition tries to seize your God-given inheritance—and it *will* happen; there's no way to prevent the attempt—will your training be enough?

The next three chapters will explore how we can live out this new and abundant life by putting on the protective equipment God has provided. Each chapter will begin with an explanation of the metaphor and the role each piece of equipment played in a Roman soldier's armor. After getting this snapshot in your mind, we'll get into the meaning of the word represented by the armor—*truth, righteousness,* or the *gospel.* Then the most critical information in each chapter will be a discussion of what this armor actually looks like in real life for ordinary people like you and me.

That's the cutting edge of our spiritual life—daily application. The key to living in victory and making the most of God's grace begins with the armor we wear.

## In Your Life

- Have you ever heard the spiritual armor described as a checklist? How would your spiritual life change if you knew that your protection was a lifestyle instead of a formula?
- Can you think of times when the enemy has exploited you at your most vulnerable moments? What weaknesses and tendencies of yours might give you a clue as to how the "evil day" applies to you?
- Is there any God-given spiritual territory you have already given up to the enemy? How can you take it back?

# 6

# Sifting through False Intelligence

Satan deals with confusion and lies. Put the truth in front of
him and he is gone.

Paul Mattock

I couldn't believe what I was hearing. Sitting across from me was a man
whose story I would have doubted except that I knew the facts firsthand.
We were talking about a crisis in his life: his marriage had fallen apart,
he was involved in an illicit relationship, and his children had rejected
him. And he was desperately depressed.

By themselves, none of those things took me by surprise. I've counseled scores of men with those exact symptoms. But their stories were
far different from his. In most cases they were either non-Christians or
nominal Christians who were not walking with God. Their lack of committed discipleship resulted in some very poor and unbiblical choices
that caused them great pain.

But this man's story was quite different. He had a godly family and a
godly heritage. He was a man of the Scriptures who had taught Sunday
school for years. He was a pillar in the church, having served on several
boards. He was the kind of man whom everyone aspired to become.

So what happened? What could possibly bring down a man with biblical convictions, a loving wife, and a successful family and business?
How could someone fall from such a blessed life to land in the depths
of despair?

The answer is sobering. In his own words, he told me: "I had it all—a beautiful wife and family, stature in the community, a significant role in the church, a thriving business, a chalet in the mountains, a condo on the beach, and all the toys you could ever imagine. I thought I was bulletproof. I thought God's hand was on me forever and that everything I touched would turn to gold. But I was wrong."

As he shared his story, he began to recount a tale of compromises in the smallest of issues: not dealing with a spat with his wife, taking that second look at a beautiful woman, telling small lies that led to bigger ones. "They all seemed so innocent and inconsequential at the time," he said. "But in a few years, they developed new patterns in my life. The lustful looks turned into a sexual addiction and then infidelity. The little lies became lapses of integrity that undermined all my relationships and destroyed my business. In very little time, I was living the opposite life of what I once had. In a word, I was deceived. Yet no matter how many people warned me, I couldn't see it. I was deceived into believing that money, sex, power, pleasure, and ego gratification were all part of the good life that I deserved and God wanted for me. I read my Bible and went to church, the truth ever before me. And I still couldn't see it. Now I'm alone, depressed, remorseful, and wishing like crazy I could do it all over. But I can't."

That isn't an uncommon deception. If we really want to learn the key to happiness—and honestly, who doesn't?—we are constantly told where we can find it. The incredible secret to realizing the meaning and joy of life is right in front of us. All we have to do is turn on the TV and watch the commercials.

Isn't that what they promise? If you want that beautiful blonde to jump into your car, you have to have the right kind of car. If you want to enjoy life to the fullest, you have to drink the right kind of beer. If you want to be a confident, influential person, you need to dye your hair this way and treat your skin that way. Nearly every advertisement gives us a glimpse into somebody's idea of what happiness is all about.

Or better yet, check out the reality shows. First we enjoyed watching houses get a makeover. Then we thought it would be interesting if people traded places and redecorated other people's houses. Then it went to trading parents and then to trading spouses. Now we can see people actually trade bodies. Shows open with someone looking one way and close with that person looking some other way—often just like a celebrity of his or her choosing.

What's behind this obsessive drive to get more, look better, and be different? What was behind the tragic fall of the man with the almost-perfect life? Lies—a subtle yet effective system of deep, dark deception.

## "Having Girded Your Loins with Truth"

The real secret to happiness isn't anywhere in prime-time entertainment, of course. The key to a fulfilled life has nothing to do with fast cars, revolving partners, or this year's fashions. Those are just counterfeits with which the enemy and the flesh conspire to tempt us. And the remedy—the number one defense against this devious deception—is to clothe ourselves in truth.

A Roman soldier had a belt, and all the rest of his armor was somehow hooked to that belt. It was critical to the rest of the equipment. If it was wintertime, soldiers wore a long robe. The first thing a soldier would do to get ready for battle was "gird up his loins." That's a weird expression—most of us don't gird up our loins when we get dressed in the morning. To a soldier, however, girding up was essential. He would lift up that long robe and tuck it into his belt so that he could move freely. On a march, he could have it down to stay warm. If he was off duty, he could unbuckle his belt. But if he was on duty and it was time for battle, an unbuckled belt and a hanging robe would mean one of two things: being punished by his superiors or having a severe disadvantage to his enemy. Either way, the consequences were grave.

So when the battle cry sounded, a soldier would lift his robe and tuck it into his belt, where his sword would hang and his shield would attach. The belt was central, and a lot depended on its being secure.

The word *truth* in this passage means candor, sincerity, and truthfulness. It is rooted in the objective reality of the truth of God's Word. Here it refers to the subjective, practical application of openness and honesty in all things with God and people.

Paul has already told us that the truth is in Christ. He has already given us three chapters of truth, assuring us of what is now true of us because of our new life in Jesus. We are accepted in him, redeemed through him, adopted into his family, and sealed with his Spirit. These things are foundational, and they have all been done for us. But putting on the belt of truth is our job. We are to train our minds to see God, ourselves, and others through the clear lens of what he says is true. That means that we don't play games. We're honest with God, honest with ourselves, and honest with others. We're open when the Spirit of God speaks to us. We don't allow ourselves to be deceived, and we don't rationalize our sins away under the disguise of ignorance, relativity, or blame.

Our first piece of armor is a direct defense against the enemy's number one tactic. Do you recall from Genesis 3 what his first attack was? Deception. Satan was the crafty serpent, dressing up his lies to make them appealing and then whispering them into Eve's ear. He deceived her by questioning God's goodness, then by questioning the accuracy of the truth of God's command. "You will not die," he said—a blatant lie. Then he quickly followed up his lie with some appealing truth. "If you eat this, it will give you the knowledge of good and evil." He was right. That was accurate. That's what Satan does; he takes truth and twists it, making sin look appealing.

Satan's modus operandi has not changed. He tells us that we'll never be happy unless we have a lot of stuff or until we look just right or until we have whatever he can get us to chase until we get it and need something more to satisfy us. The dissatisfactions deep within us—the very cravings that all those advertisements exploit—are the products of his lies. He convinces us we need more and more and more, and then he tempts us to get it in ungodly ways. And before we know it, we're buying the lies—hook, line, and sinker.

Have you noticed that? We can go to church on Sundays, read the Bible in the morning, pray our daily prayers, and still unconsciously let the media so infiltrate our thinking that we raise our kids just about the same way the world raises their kids and handle our money about the same way that the world does. That's what those pesky surveys by Gallup and Barna keep telling us. The fact is that the average Christian in America is strikingly similar to the non-Christian in the way we talk, act, and live. The level of honesty among Christians and the level of honesty in American culture at large are not much different. Why? We're deceived.

We don't know we're deceived, of course. I don't know many people running around saying, "I'm a deceived Christian. I don't really know what's going on. I get suckered every day in every way." When we're deceived, we're deceived. We think we're right on target. We're convinced we're doing the right things for the right reasons and with the right motives. Eve didn't bite the forbidden fruit while thinking to herself, "This is really going to be bad news." She thought she was making a wise decision, and the first bite probably tasted great. God had made it, after all. But she ate it based on lies, and she didn't even know it.

We tend to believe a lot of lies. Read the following examples and see if they don't sound all too familiar:

- Take care of yourself first and foremost. No one else will. (The American way, right?)
- The Bible was written centuries ago, and it's just not relevant anymore in some areas. (Besides, you'll look like an anti-intellectual fool if you defend the Bible in this day and age.)

- Truth is relative. What's true for you may not be true for me. (*Tolerance* is the word of the day. And who are you to say what's right for everyone else anyway?)
- Stand up for your rights. The Bible says not to sue your brother in Christ, but it's probably justifiable in this situation. (Have you heard the news reports of Christian leaders suing other Christian leaders—even though the Bible says it is better to be defrauded than to defame the church and the name of God?)
- We love each other. God understands that we have hormones and drives we can't control. Besides, we plan to get married soon anyway.

Satan's first attack was deception, and humanity's first response after sin was hiding, denial, and blame-shifting. That hasn't changed much either, has it? When we see the truth about ourselves, it's painful. It takes a lot of courage to face up to reality. It's easier for us to go into denial or to point a finger at someone else. We are very creative blame-shifters. We attribute our sinful reactions to difficult circumstances, a depressed economy, an unfaithful spouse, or anything or anyone other than ourselves.

The remedy is the belt of truth. Whoever or whatever we blame may actually be at fault to some extent in our situation, but until we get honest with God and with each other, we are playing with deception. Kenneth Wuest writes that the belt of truth is evident in the man or woman whose mind "will practice no deceit and no disguises in our intercourse with God."[4] We need to own up to our own faults without excuses and without blaming, bring them to God, and confess them honestly before him. That's the only way to stand firm against deception.

I remember my first experience of not having the belt of truth on and being clueless about it. (There have been many, by the way.) As I was growing up, my father—who had been a Marine—drilled his life principles into me. "Son, this is how life works. Some people get up early, and some people get up late. So get up early. Some people set goals, and some people don't. So set goals. Some people develop strategies and go for their goals; some people don't. So develop strategies and go for it. Some people want it bad enough; some people don't. So do whatever it takes to do the job and accomplish the goal." The underlying assumption to all these messages—the lie that was taught to him and passed down to me—was that this is the way to be successful, and if you're successful, you'll be happy.

By seventh grade I was an emerging workaholic. I had written goals for the kind of girl I wanted to date, what I would achieve in basketball and baseball, how I would earn good grades and make the honor roll, and how I would win a scholarship. I got up early, I set my goals, and I developed my strategies. By the time I was a senior, I had realized about 90 percent of them. One of the reasons I came to Christ was that God used a close friend to expose the lie by giving me a great compliment: "Wow, you've really got it made," she said, and she began to list all my "successes." As the words came out of her mouth, I realized I *did* "have it made" in a way—the way the world measures success. But at that moment I also realized that the formula didn't work because I was the emptiest guy on the face of the earth—and the phoniest guy too, because I had learned to develop relationships through self-centered strategies.

Shortly after that experience, I came to know Jesus in a personal way, and I was liberated. It was powerful and transforming. Someone gave me a Bible, and I just about devoured it. It seemed like whoever wrote it had been reading my thoughts and was speaking directly to me. A lot of my old goals were no longer attractive, and God began to give me new desires. I wanted to be his man. I went away to college and met a group of people who were great at discipling people like me, and I soon found myself whistling and singing and enjoying spending time with God.

But just because you go from the kingdom of darkness to the kingdom of light doesn't mean everything negative goes away overnight. I found that people in this Christian group really liked you a lot if you could memorize a lot of Bible verses, so I memorized twice as many as everyone else. They recommended being in a Bible study, so I decided not just to be in one but to lead one. I followed a rigid list of rules and never missed a day of prayer. I hung out with all the spiritual people on campus, and after about two years I lost my joy. I forgot all about the wonder and delight of my new relationship with Jesus. I became a legalistic Pharisee who knew a lot of verses but had no joy, a super-Christian who had no compassion for people. I was new in Christ, but I defaulted to my earlier principles: get up early, set goals, make strategies, and want it more than everyone else. The belt of truth was not on anymore. I was deceived.

Tragically, I was getting rewarded for my deception in this little campus ministry subculture. People would say, "Do you know Chip? He knows a lot of verses, he never misses a day of prayer time, and he shares his faith with everything that moves." That only reinforced my legalism. Then I reconnected with a girl I had met in my first year at college, and the conversation was brief, but I'll remember it forever. She looked at me and said out of the blue, "You know, Chip, I remember your first year here. You were a really neat guy. You just seemed so happy, and while I've never been real high on Christians, you made me think there might be something to it. But you've changed. Anytime I hear you, all you have is verses for people. All you have now is religion. If this is what it is like to be a Christian, I don't think I'd ever want to be one. See you later."

I was stunned. In fact, I was devastated. I felt like someone had walked up to me out of the blue and punched me in the stomach. Here I was, trying to be the best Christian I could be, only to learn I was turning off those I was trying to reach. She made me realize the difference between who I had been and who I became. It was just the slap in the face I needed to get me to stop and take a hard look at what abundant life is all about. My armor had not been on. I wasn't wearing the belt of truth. I had taken all of my old thinking and translated it into the Christian world, trying to achieve success, security, and significance based on my performance of the disciplines of the Christian life. I was deceived into believing people would love and accept me only if I were a super-Christian.

That was twenty-five years ago, but I find that nearly every week as I spend time with God, I'm being deceived in some way that requires my putting the belt of truth back on. I'll realize that I haven't been exactly honest or open with some people or that I haven't quite been honest with God. And the Word of God will have to wash over my heart once again, because that's the mirror that lets me know what reality is.

You don't just put on the belt of truth in a quiet time some morning or with a quick prayer in the car. It's a process. It comes through long, significant seasons of being with God, not out of duty but out of longing to hear his voice. It comes when we stop ignoring that uncomfortable lack of peace, that disquieting voice in the back of our minds, and refuse to cover it up. Our tendency is to put on a movie or turn on some music whenever we're alone because God's voice is easier to ignore that way. We don't like to hear it because we're being deceived. And for many of us, it has been a very long time since we unzipped our heart and said, "Lord, show me anything in me that doesn't line up with who you are."

So how about you? Where has your belt of truth slipped? In what ways are you blaming others, playing games, and hiding from God?

For years, I would hide for days at a time when I knew things weren't right with God. I assumed he would be mad at me for not coming clean. That's the deception. God is not a cosmic cop but a loving Father. I've learned that the moment I stop, really get honest, and come clean with God, I meet a loving, forgiving God who is full of grace and mercy and who wants to restore my sense of peace and bring integrity to all of my relationships.

That can happen only after we are honest—only when we're willing to put on the belt of truth and live with openness and humility. When we do, something painful but wonderful occurs. It's called brokenness. That is when we see the truth about who we really are.

When I saw how hypocritical I was, and how far from Christlikeness I was, I literally wept. And I still have to do some of that. I'll write to God in my journal about how I postured myself in a meeting that day in order to appear confident or impress people or how I see some arrogance coming into my relationship with my family or my colleagues. Defensiveness occurs when God brings truth into our lives and we won't receive it. We justify ourselves rather than confess the reality of our faults. So I'm learning to put on the belt of truth and let it break my heart. That's okay. Psalm 34:18 says, "The LORD is near to the brokenhearted and saves those who are crushed in spirit." The Spirit of God is always a friend of truth, especially when it hurts.

### Personal Application: What about You?

David, we are told, was a man after God's own heart, but that doesn't mean he had it all together, does it? He wasn't always the epitome of moral righteousness. So what made him a man after God's heart? When David was confronted with his sin, it broke him. After his sin with Bathsheba, he did what we all do: denial, blame-shifting, and cover-up. But when God brought Nathan the prophet to David to help him see the truth, it broke his heart. We have the record of his repentance in Psalm 51, but I think we see some of the fruit of his repentance in Psalm 139.

David learned to keep short accounts with God, and he learned that knowing the truth—even if it was painful—was the best way to do that. In verses 23–24 of Psalm 139, David prayed: "Search me, O God, and know my heart; try me and know my anxious thoughts; and see if there be any hurtful way in me. And lead me in the everlasting way." That is a really good prayer to pray every day. "Lord, search me. As far as I know, I'm right with you and my other relationships are okay, but I want to know if I'm being deceived." Then when God speaks, listen. He won't speak in vague condemnations: "You're a bad person," "You need to be a better parent," and generalities like that. He will convict you about specific things for which you can repent. His desire is never to condemn and always to draw you back into intimate relationship with himself.

### In Your Life

- Do you know people who get defensive when God (or someone else) points out the truth? Do you do that yourself? What does that indicate about their (or your) spiritual armor?

- It is often said that everyone wears a mask. In other words, insecurity drives us all to posture and pose in certain situations to make a good impression on others. How can the truth of our position in Christ help us take off our mask?
- Can you think of a past experience in which God pointed out some deception in your life? How did you apply his truth to that situation?
- Would your relationship with God change if you prayed Psalm 139:23–24 every day? In what ways?

# 7

# In Sync with God

The demons say one thing to get us into sin, and another to
overwhelm us in despair.

John Climacus

One of my colleagues spent the first decade of his ministry under an
extremely heavy burden. He loved and served God, but it was never
enough. There were always more souls to save, more mouths to feed,
more wounds to heal, and more conflicts to resolve. And woe to him if
he rested in the midst of such crying need. God had a zealous agenda,
and my friend dared not neglect it.

That may sound like the hard labor of a servant-hearted saint, but
there was a lot of guilt behind it. When my friend shares how he came
to Christ, the joy of salvation is only a small part of the story. Almost
immediately after his conversion, he began to see God as a hard taskmaster who was angry with his people for still not getting the gospel to the
entire planet, even after two thousand years. This man worked for God
because God required it and because he felt extraordinarily guilty if he
didn't. He served out of obligation and fear—a dread of the condemnation that would come if he slacked off—rather than out of love and joy.
He was motivated by an overbearing sense of painful duty.

That's a common condition among earnest Christians. Some people
spend their whole lives going to church because they would feel guilty
if they didn't. They give money not because they long to be involved in
eternal work and to bless people but because they know they are supposed

to. They volunteer when asked because they will condemn themselves if they don't. Or they don't volunteer at all because they just live with condemnation all the time.

Guilt plays out in our lives in very warped ways. It is often at the root of dysfunctional families, eating disorders, sexual addictions, and addictions to drugs and alcohol. More subtly, though, it's just a whisper from the enemy that says, "You call yourself a Christian, but if anyone knew all the things you do—those secret sins behind closed doors, the way you hide your insecurities with clothes and surgeries, the emotional dysfunction you inflict on others—they'd keep their distance from you. A Christian? You'd be exposed as a fraud! God isn't going to hear your prayers. He isn't even going to take you back. You've failed him too many times." Guilt is a killer.

It doesn't take long for us to be smothered in condemnation. It isn't that we aren't truly guilty. Some people deny that there is such a thing as guilt—no morals, no consequences, no problem. No, guilt is real. But so is forgiveness, and God's grace is greater not only than all our sin but also than all our guilt. Satan's first mode of attack was deception, but he follows it up with heavy doses of condemnation. And the second piece of armor we need to put in place will protect us from it perfectly.

### "Having Put on the Breastplate of Righteousness"

A Roman breastplate was usually made of bronze, or, if you were a more affluent soldier, chain mail. It covered the midsection and then some, from just below the neck to the thighs. And they called it a heart protector—for obvious reasons. It guarded the vital organ that keeps us alive.

That's what Paul tells us to put on after we've girded ourselves up in the belt of truth. The next piece of equipment is the heart protector—the breastplate of righteousness. No one would dare go into battle without it.

What exactly does *righteousness* mean? You may be tempted to give up if you think it means you have to become perfect before you can be protected, but don't give up just yet. That's not what this is about. The word *righteousness* in Ephesians 6:14 means "uprightness, right living, integrity in one's lifestyle and character." It is a matter of conforming our will to God's will. It is rooted in the objective righteousness that we already possess in our standing before God through Christ's work. That righteousness cannot be taken away. It is complete because we are in Christ and he is in us. But while the righteousness of this verse flows out of that objective reality, this is really the practical application of truth to our lives. In other words, the righteousness referred to here is submitting to the lordship of Christ. Put simply, it's putting into practice what you know is right.

That's why the belt of truth came first. We have to have that. It is fundamental. Now that we have it, though, we need to apply it. That's what righteousness is. It is putting into practice what God has told us through his Word, his community, and his worship. We can immerse ourselves in Scripture and spiritual fellowship all we want to, but if those things don't transform the way we live, they are practically useless. When God works his truth into our hearts, we are called to live it out 24/7.

## Accusations That Wound

There's a reason Satan is called the accuser of the brethren (Rev. 12:10). When we fall into sin, the Holy Spirit will convict us and draw us through repentance and forgiveness back into fellowship with the Father. But Satan will counterfeit the conviction with accusations. The whisper who laughs, "You call yourself a Christian?" is not the voice of the Holy Spirit. That's demonic, and it is designed to drive you into false comforts to ease your guilt. For example, buying seventy-five pairs of shoes because when it's too painful to face the truth and you feel condemned, shopping will give you an adrenaline rush to take care of it—for a while. Or stuffing yourself in order to drown your pain in pleasure—and then throwing it all up as you kick yourself for being so addicted to food. Or becoming the dispenser of personal information in your congregation because you need to feel significant. It's all in the form of prayer requests, of course. "Mr. and Mrs. So-and-so are going through a difficult time in their marriage. You heard what she did, didn't you? They need lots of prayer." "Pray for that family that has been visiting. Did you know they had to disconnect the cable because their kids got into some of those perverted sexual issues?" Eventually, you become the garbage can of the church. But you feel significant, and it eases your conscience. Almost all of these games we play are designed to muffle the enemy's accusations.

The breastplate of righteousness is essential when we have been honest with God, accepted his revealed will (the belt of truth), and then put into practice what he has told us. The condemnation comes, and we stand our ground and say, "That's a lie, Satan. I'm complete in Christ." Or, if there's truth to his accusation, "That's a lie, Satan. That *was* true—I really was a phony. But I'm not anymore because 1 John 1:9 is true: if I confess my sins, God is faithful and just to forgive my sin and cleanse me of all unrighteousness. Did you get that? *All* unrighteousness." You stand your ground because you believe what God tells you. You are complete in Christ, you are pure in him, and you reject the trash-talking that evil, demonic whisper is spouting off at you. When he tells you that food will soothe your discomfort, expensive purchases will ease the pain, or sexual satisfaction—however you can get it, moral or not—will make you feel all better, put the truth into practice. "I have real intimacy; I don't need that. I know the source of real satisfaction; I'm not going to play any more games." Satan's accusations and heavy loads of guilt and shame cannot pierce the breastplate of righteousness. In Christ we are righteous, and in practice, we are being conformed to his image.

Do you detect a sense of urgency in this? I hope so. The time to feel victimized and overwhelmed is over. We are not victims of our compulsions. The whispers telling you to try harder (so that you'll fall harder when you fail) are not the Holy Spirit. God doesn't want you to try harder. He wants you to apply the truth now, rely on the power you presently possess, and by faith put on the breastplate of righteousness. You do *not* have to live where the condemnations of your heart take you.

Here's what it looks like when we do not put on the breastplate of righteousness—in other words, when we willfully rebel against the truth God has shown us. We open ourselves to demonic attack. That's the implication, isn't it? We are to put on the breastplate as part of our protection against the enemy's attacks. If we don't put it on, the result is vulnerability to his attacks. We open ourselves up to full frontal assault from the spirits of darkness.

## Biblical Examples of Breastplate Malfunctions

Does that seem too strong? If so, let's take a look at what Scripture has to say about it. In 1 Samuel 13, Saul, the first king of Israel, heard God's instructions through the priest Samuel. Saul was about to go into battle against the Philistines, but first he was to wait at Gilgal for seven days until Samuel arrived to offer a sacrifice to God. But seven days passed, and the enemy was gathering. The men were afraid, morale was low, and some of the troops were beginning to scatter. Saul took matters into his own hands, deciding it was better to please his men than to please God. He made the sacrifice himself and then rationalized his behavior. From the moment he disobeyed what he knew was true, he opened the door to demonic activity in his life.

That tendency to disobey turned up again and again. Two chapters later, Saul understood God's truth: he was to go to battle against the Amalekites, put them all to death, and destroy everything that belonged to them—including their livestock. But he turned away from truth and chose self-sufficiency over God-dependence. Saul obeyed most of God's instructions, but not all of them. He spared the Amalekite king and the best of the sheep and cattle (1 Sam. 15:8–9).

God rejected Saul as king because of these two incidents, and for the rest of Saul's reign, he was consumed with jealousy and fits of insanity. Demonic activity pursued him relentlessly as he lost touch with reality and turned inward, growing bitter and vengeful toward people who had done him no wrong. His moods swung up and down, and his relationships crumbled. Saul was a king without a breastplate of righteousness, and he lost the battle.

This dynamic isn't confined to the Old Testament. Jesus asked his disciples a question one day: "Who do people say that the Son of Man is?" (Matt. 16:13). His disciples gave him a quick summary of popular opinion on Jesus's identity. Then Jesus asked, "Who do *you* say that I am?" Peter, who didn't exactly say the right things at the right times, nailed this one. "You are the Christ, the Son of the living God" (v. 16). Jesus told Peter that this was a revelation of the Holy Spirit and that Peter did a great job seeing the spiritual reality of Jesus's identity. He even blessed Peter as "the Rock" and declared that he would build his church on this truth. Then Jesus went on to tell the disciples the rest of the game plan. He would go to the cross, suffer, and die and then be raised. Peter, just off of one of history's most Spirit-inspired declarations, rebuked Jesus for such ridiculous notions. "God forbid it, Lord! This shall never happen to You." Jesus's response is brutal but accurate: "Get behind Me, Satan. You are a stumbling block to Me" (vv. 22–23). Peter had heard the truth from the Son of God's mouth, rebelled against it, and opened the door to a statement straight from Satan.

### What's in Your Heart?

Consider this question carefully before you answer it: in what area of your life has God spoken his truth to you that you are not currently following? Are you deceived? There are Christians reading this book who resemble me in college—a first-class Pharisee. Others of you head a ministry at your church, read your Bible every morning, listen to radio preachers, pray for your friends, family, and ministries, and yet you are still walking in deception. You may have anger fantasies about your ex-spouse, even though the Bible has some really clear things to say about bitterness. You may not have spoken with someone in the church for five years because of some past offense, even though the Bible is very clear that we are to forgive others the way God has forgiven us. You may not give very much of your time, your talents, or your treasure, even though the Bible is emphatic about giving the first portion of your resources to the Lord. For others, the duplicity reveals itself in little or no concern for those who are perishing outside of Christ, even though the Bible commands us to build bridges according to the way God has made us in order to bring people out of darkness into the kingdom of light. We are people of flesh, and we all grow deaf to God's clear instructions from time to time while fully convinced we are following them completely. That's deception; it results in unrighteousness, and that leads to vulnerability in the face of demonic attack.

Have you opened your heart to demonic activity in any of these ways? I'm not suggesting that your bed is going to start shaking, that you'll have visions and weird phenomena coming at you, or that you'll fly into a jealous rage like Saul. You will, however, miss out on the abundant life God has given you if you are constantly living under condemnation and guilt. So many of us go on for years clueless about what's missing in our spiritual lives, only to one day realize we have been ignoring God's clear instructions to us. Listen carefully: an unprotected heart is asking for deep, life-threatening wounds.

Many of you just got nailed with some sharply pointed truth. You may be going right to that place we talked about at the beginning of this chapter: guilt and condemnation. "Money . . . forgiveness . . . sharing my faith . . . deception and demonic attack. Ouch." Before you wallow in shame, let me encourage you. We all do these things. The solution isn't condemnation; it's restoring our honesty with God and allowing him to clothe us in his righteousness in practical ways. Matthew 6:33 says to seek first the kingdom of God and *his* righteousness. That means we make time for God every day. And he understands days that are crazy—this isn't a legalistic requirement. It just means that he is to matter most to us. He is our most important relationship, evidenced not by our lips but by our lives. And if he isn't, we have a breastplate to put on. We know the truth; all that's left is to follow it.

Does that mean you have to be perfect? Of course not. It means you deal with the areas God has shown you. If he has shown you that you watch too much TV, then scale back. If he has shown you a bad habit with food, break it. If he has shown you some issues in your marriage that you can't resolve outside of counseling, then get a counselor. Just do it. Whatever God has shown you, regardless of your fear, take the first step. Once you do, he'll give you grace. The first time you give back to him off the top of your income, he'll give you grace. The first time you forgive someone whom you really don't want to forgive, he'll be there to fill your heart with grace. Change your schedule, your diet, your goals in life—if he has shown you to do something, he will give you power and grace to do it. The breastplate of righteousness is not that difficult to put on when God is helping us.

If we aren't wearing the breastplate of righteousness, our hearts are being condemned by the enemy and our minds are being deceived. Instead of our lives reflecting the supernatural, winsome love and holiness of Jesus, we are religious people working hard to please God and impress people in our own strength. That's a heavy burden to bear. We can't do it ourselves, and God doesn't want us to. He wants to help us walk in his truth and his righteousness and guard ourselves against the enemy's deceptions and accusations. And grace—that "will to," "want to," and "power to"—is always abundant when he is our first priority.

**Personal Application: What about You?**

James 4:17 says, "To the one who knows the right thing to do and does not do it, to him it is sin." The fruit we bite into against God's instructions is sweet on the front end—there is an initial reward when someone clicks on that porn site, takes food he or she doesn't need, or harbors resentment. But it is bitter fruit to swallow. It will destroy us. Not just hurt us; destroy us.

A chapter on righteousness can easily end up with a legalistic flavor to it. I know that. That's not what this is about. Every command God gives you is for your own good because he loves you. These instructions flow from a concerned Father's heart. His promise is that you can know the truth, and the truth will set you free (John 8:32). God gave you rules about priorities, money, bitterness, relationships, purity, and all aspects of your life not because he wants to burden you with restrictions but because he wants you to get his very best. He wants you to have real peace, not artificial peace that comes from eating, shopping, or vacationing. He wants you to have a clean heart and experience his power, not brief moments of holding problems at bay. The last thing he wants is for you to self-destruct. He does not want you standing in the middle of an invisible war without any protection over your heart. The breastplate of righteousness—your righteousness in Christ working out practically in your life—is a God-given safeguard. Put it on every day, moment by moment. And wear it well.

**In Your Life**

- What activities and responsibilities do you fulfill out of a sense of guilt? What steps can you take to remove the sense of guilt and replace it with a devotion to God?

- How can you tell the difference between the Holy Spirit's conviction and the enemy's condemnation?
- The thought that rebellion opens us up to demonic attack is frightening—and sometimes hard to swallow. What would you tell someone who thinks that obedience is not really a big deal to God?
- Is there anything God has shown you to do that you are not currently doing (or that he has shown you not to do that you are currently doing)? If so, what?
- What statement does our disobedience make about our relationship with God?

# 8

# Bombarded by Doubts

The devil can counterfeit all the saving operations and graces of the Spirit of God.

Jonathan Edwards

The first year of my Christian life was one of the most delightful and difficult times I can remember. My new relationship with Christ brought a freedom that I had never experienced. I found myself singing and whistling or just plain being happy in ways I had never experienced before. To be accepted just as I was, to be forgiven absolutely and completely, and to know that God wanted to speak to me every day in the Scriptures was almost more than I could take.

But along with the new delight were some grave difficulties. I didn't grow up in a Bible-teaching church or home. I came to know Christ only a few months before I went away to college. I was reading the Bible on my own because I couldn't put it down, but I didn't have a clue as to how this new life in Christ was to be lived.

I couldn't explain why things were happening inside of me. I just knew that they were. I didn't realize the Holy Spirit had come into my life and that since he is holy, he was creating holy desires within me. My friends couldn't understand when I didn't want to go barhopping with them anymore. I'm not sure I could understand it myself, except it just wasn't fun anymore, and it made me feel dirty. Those kinds of changes were encouraging, but some things didn't change very easily at all.

Though I didn't know a lot of the Bible, I knew that swearing and using God's name in vain were not things I wanted to do anymore. Yet time after time, I found myself slipping into old patterns and hearing things come out of my mouth that made me feel guilty and ashamed. I also knew that using and manipulating people for personal gain—especially girls—was out of bounds with God. Yet I found myself repeatedly defaulting to my old ways. I felt such shame that I wondered if I really had a relationship with Christ.

I didn't know it at the time, but the enemy was whispering those doubts in my heart on a regular basis. It may sound funny now, but I probably asked Christ to come into my life at least twenty times that first year. I didn't understand my position in him or how his grace dealt with my sin and failure. I was always doubting, always unsure, and always living with piles of condemnation and overwhelming guilt. I came close to giving up—in fact, I once officially decided to quit the Christian life—because I couldn't stand being a hypocrite. I almost fell into Satan's trap. I was within an inch of becoming a casualty to the enemy's bombardment of doubt. I almost lost my footing.

### "Having Shod Your Feet with the Preparation of the Gospel of Peace"

Roman sandals were strapped up to the knee and tightly fastened to the soldier's leg. The soles had knobs and sometimes nails protruding from them—an ancient version of athletic cleats. Alexander the Great is said to have invented these or at least championed them. He gave credit for many of the Greek army's impressive victories to the firm footing of its forces. When soldiers have a solid foundation, they can stand unmoved against their opposition. They don't slip or lose their balance very often if their feet are gripping the ground.

That's the picture Paul wants us to have of ourselves: soldiers with feet solidly planted in certainty. That's also the picture any athletic coach wants his players to envision. When I used to coach basketball, I would tell my kids to bend their knees and get down. To play defense well, they had to keep a low center of gravity for balance and footing. They hated to do it, but they couldn't defend unless they got down low. A wide receiver in football has a lot of trouble when the turf is slick or his cleats are not long enough. Why? Because you can't make a sharp cut if you don't have a firm foundation. We even apply this principle to our toddlers. When they are learning to walk, we don't make it hard for them by putting them in socks on smooth, hardwood floors. We put them on a carpet or dress them in slippers with rubber grips on the bottom so they won't get hurt. If footing is crucial in sports and childhood, how much more crucial is it in the high-stakes, life-or-death, invisible war?

Imagine putting on the belt of truth to guard against Satan's deceptions and the breastplate of righteousness to guard against his condemnation. Your vital organs are protected. But what good will that do you if you can't keep your footing? You have to be able to support all of your equipment with the kind of foundation that will allow you to keep your backside off the ground.

The word *preparation* in this verse means "establishment." It conveys two ideas: knowing the gospel inside and out and being ready to share it. When we are well grounded in the mercy of God in Christ and are prepared to extend his mercy to others, we are on solid ground. That kind of readiness brings peace on both fronts—within our own hearts and between God and people who need him.

We've discovered that Satan's primary tactic is deception, and he follows it up with condemnation. The belt of truth and the breastplate of righteousness guard us from those tactics. But he also specializes in casting doubt on the very basis of God's goodness and the means by which we receive it: the gospel. He always attacks grace.

My daughter had a friend who had fallen victim to that attack. This Christian friend was convinced that no one could really be sure of making it to heaven. You just do your best and hope, she believed. That's the approach of a lot of false gospels, of which there is no shortage in this world. The paths of many other religions are steep and winding, demanding perfection from their travelers. The natural tendency of a fallen human being is to rely on good works and to push all the right buttons to possibly have a chance of getting to heaven. When that self-oriented approach to God seeps into a Christian's life, it's hard to recover. If grace has been undermined in a believer's mind, self is all that is left—hope in our own resources.

But when failure comes, like it did in my life, then the only conclusion one can draw is, "Maybe I don't really belong to Christ." And if we can never really know, we become a pawn in the hand of the enemy—forever plagued by doubts about our worthiness before God. We revert to a performance orientation, and when our self-effort fails, the result is often that we are tempted to give up—which I almost did. Few things will undermine joy and abundance in a Christian life as much as that.

This is the "different gospel" that Paul addressed in Galatians: "I am amazed that you are so quickly deserting Him who called you by the grace of Christ, for a different gospel; which is *really* not another. . . . Even if we, or an angel from heaven, should preach to you a gospel contrary to what we have preached to you, he is to be accursed!" (Gal. 1:6–8). Later in the same letter, Paul calls the Galatians fools. They had begun in the

Spirit and then thought they could be Christians by human effort. They had fallen for a lie (Gal. 3:1–14).

Satan loves to cast doubt by offering another gospel—another Jesus or another way to salvation. Jesus may be a part of the scheme, but not as the Son of God who paid it all. That makes the false gospel even more deceptive. Jesus is in the middle of it, but his atoning work is ignored. Satan adds to the gospel of grace through faith, making it a gospel of grace through faith plus works. And then he convinces us we've never done quite enough works.

The tactic of another gospel is the essence of 2 Corinthians 11:3–4. Satan comes to us as an angel of light. He makes the lie look good. It seems to be Christian or deeply spiritual or charitable and compassionate, and it's usually mixed with a whole lot of truth. But it's still a lie. And Satan offers his alternatives right after he lays the groundwork with his whispering doubts. "You don't really believe all this, do you? I mean, the God who created the entire universe becoming a man, living a perfect life, dying on a cross, and then being resurrected? You have to give the first portion of your hard-earned money to a church full of sinners, and you have to live a boring, righteous life in a world that's having a lot more fun. When are you going to quit playing these games and stop falling for this religious garbage? You don't need that crutch anymore. After all, you're an educated person. This is what they spoon-feed to the gullible and ignorant. Is that what you want to be?" Satan wants us to fall for an easier gospel, a prettier gospel, or a more socially respectable gospel. Can you see how you must have a firm foundation when you hear that voice?

The solution is pretty simple. It is to immerse ourselves in the fundamentals and foundations of the Christian faith as it is revealed to us in the Bible. God's Word is very clear that we are sinners in need of salvation, and we cannot help ourselves. But he sent his Son into the world to live a perfect life and to die as the full payment for our sin. God's holiness and our guilt have been satisfied completely. By faith, we accept the sacrifice of the Son of God and live by the power of his Spirit. That's the gospel, and there is no other. That is what we strap on our feet and drive deep into the turf, and it is on this that we stand our ground.

## Personal Application: What about You?

What does that look like in our lives? First and foremost, we need to know and understand the gospel clearly, as concretely as it is presented in 1 Corinthians 15:1–6 and Ephesians 2:1–9.

I make known to you, brethren, the gospel which I preached to you, which also you received, in which also you stand, by which also you are saved, if you hold fast the word which I preached to you, unless you believed in vain. For I delivered to you as of first importance what I also received, that Christ died for our sins according to the Scriptures, and that He was buried, and that He was raised on the third day according to the Scriptures, and that He appeared to Cephas, then to the twelve. After that He appeared to more than five hundred brethren at one time.

1 Corinthians 15:1–6

There is nothing ambiguous about that. Paul presents a gospel that is rooted in space-time history. This is not a dream, not a religion, and not just one option among many on the religious salad bar. It is not possible to believe this gospel and then conclude that we are left to find peace and fulfillment in some out-of-body journey or wherever we can find it. This is about a real-life, historical figure. Paul dared his readers to check it out for themselves, and he told them that if this gospel was not verifiable, the Christian faith was in vain (1 Cor. 15:14). This bold claim is entirely dependent on objective reality, not subjective experience. The Good News—and that's what *gospel* actually means—is that Jesus died on a cross to pay for our sins in full, and those who trust him are forgiven and absolutely clean. The power of sin is broken, Satan has been defeated, and Jesus has made us free.

Second, we need to know the basis for our eternal security and the assurance of our salvation. If you are ever feeling insecure about your salvation, read Romans 8:38–39: "I am convinced that neither death, nor life, nor angels, nor principalities, nor things present, nor things to come, nor powers, nor height, nor depth, nor any other created thing, will be able to separate us from the love of God, which is in Christ Jesus our Lord." And if you ever need heavy doses of assurance, spend some time in 1 John 5:11–13: "The testimony is this, that God has given us eternal life, and this life is in His Son. He who has the Son has the life; he who does not have the Son of God does not have the life. These things I have written to you who believe in the name of the Son of God, so that you may know that you have eternal life." Ephesians 1:13–14 promises us that God's Spirit has sealed us and made us God's own possession.

My daughter's friend could have found a lot of peace in these passages. So could a young man I once met. He was in a college singing group that traveled to churches to give concerts during which group members would share their testimonies. I was standing next to him after a concert in our church, and he said he wanted to ask me a question. So we talked a little bit, and it turned out that he was really struggling with doubt. He was weighed down by guilt and condemnation—the breastplate of righteousness could have prevented that—and as a result, he was seriously questioning his salvation. Here was a guy who had been doing Christian work for years, and he was completely paralyzed by overwhelming doubts, wondering whether he was in the faith or not. His foundation was slipping. His feet were not securely shod with the preparation of the gospel of peace.

I can relate. When I've been traveling a lot, living on two or three hours of sleep each night, and then run into a difficult time or a conflict with someone I care about, I don't really feel like reading the Bible or praying. Fatigue, stress, and discouragement can make anyone feel very un-Christian. It can happen to anyone at any time. I've even felt that way on overseas trips specifically to teach other people about Jesus. Then the whisperer gets in my ear: "You have just been telling thousands of people about Jesus, and you don't want to read your Bible or pray? You're a real phony, aren't you?"

That's a really good time to remember that faith is based on facts—the objective reality of the gospel of peace—rather than on feelings. You can eat a bad enchilada and have some negative feelings. Feelings come and go. But the gospel is rooted in truth, and we have to be able to tell the enemy that we know we are saved because we believe in the gospel of Jesus Christ, which is hard, rock-solid fact. Our momentary mood does not tell us whether or not we are in the faith.

Finally, I want to encourage you to do something that will powerfully strengthen your faith and help you become established. It may seem threatening at first, but ask God for specific opportunities to share your faith. Telling the gospel to others is one of the most amazing faith-builders available—or, as they say, the best defense is a good offense. You don't have to be a passionate evangelist on the order of Billy Graham or Luis Palau. As you identify with Christ, you can share your faith according to your gifts and personality when the opportunity arises.

The most vibrant time I ever had in terms of my confidence in God's goodness was when I played basketball overseas with some other Christian college players. We played throughout South America. On a slow day I would share the gospel ten times, and on a good day, twice that. Paul wrote in Romans 1:16 that he was not ashamed of the gospel because it was the power of God for salvation, and that power is felt not only by the one who hears it but also by the one who shares it. You can be tired and worn out, but when you see the supernatural message being used by God again and again, you suddenly realize that you are part of something powerful and eternal. That summer as I shared my faith time after time, it became natural. I realized that the power wasn't in the messenger but in the message.

As you share the gospel, you will realize that the foundation of your faith is strong, clear, and intellectually defensible. Doubt will begin to disappear. Your shoes will become more deeply and firmly planted in the ground.

## In Your Life

- Have you noticed at which times in your life you are most likely to question God's goodness? Why do these times leave you vulnerable to doubt?
- How much does your faith depend on your feelings? When you notice your faith coming and going with your mood, what steps can you take to ground yourself more firmly in the gospel?
- Practice sharing your faith with someone before answering the following question. (If that's scary for you, start with a believer you know well and who will encourage you.) Did your confidence in the gospel increase or decrease when you shared your faith? Why?

## What You Need to Remember

God has objectively defeated Satan and his agenda. He has delivered us from sin's penalty and power, and ultimately he will deliver us from sin's very presence. In the interim, we are involved in guerrilla warfare with demonic forces.

As believers, we have been transferred from the kingdom of darkness to the kingdom of light, with all the rights, privileges, and position that being a child of God entails. The spiritual battle we fight involves a responsibility on our part to put on the spiritual protection that God has provided for us. We can and will resist the enemy's attempts to deceive, accuse, and cast doubt when we stand firm against him by:

1. being honest with God, ourselves, and others as a prerequisite to all spiritual battle,
2. responding to the truth that God shows us about his will for our lives—righteous living,
3. clearly understanding the gospel and habitually sharing this message of grace.

The great majority of spiritual warfare need never go beyond the regular practice of living out our position in Christ by faith. Our practice of Paul's metaphor of the spiritual armor protects us from Satan's ongoing attempts to break our fellowship with Jesus and, as a result, greatly minimizes any impact by the enemy.

There are times, however, when we must move beyond standing firm and engage the enemy in actual combat. This will be the topic of section 3 (Eph. 6:16–17).

# Spiritual Warfare 301

## How to Do Battle with the Enemy and Win

Anyone who witnesses to the grace of God revealed in Christ is undertaking direct assault against Satan's dominion.

Thomas Cosmades

In addition to all, [take] up the shield of faith with which you will be able to extinguish all the flaming arrows of the evil one. And take the helmet of salvation, and the sword of the Spirit, which is the word of God.

Ephesians 6:16–17

## Introduction: Advanced Training

**Review: Four Facts You Need to Know**

1. God has objectively defeated Satan and his agenda. He has delivered us from sin's penalty and power, and ultimately he will deliver us from sin's very presence. In the interim, we are involved in guerrilla warfare with demonic forces.
2. As believers, we have been transferred from the kingdom of darkness to the kingdom of light, with all the rights, privileges, and position that being a child of God entails.
3. The spiritual battle we fight involves a responsibility on our part to put on the spiritual protection that God has provided for us. We can and will resist the enemy's attempts to deceive, accuse, and cast doubt when we stand firm against him by:
   a. being honest with God, ourselves, and others as a prerequisite to all spiritual battle,
   b. responding to the truth that God shows us about his will for our lives—righteous living,
   c. clearly understanding and readily sharing the gospel message of grace.
4. The great majority of spiritual warfare need never go beyond the regular practice of living out our position in Christ by faith. Our practice of Paul's metaphor of the spiritual armor protects us from Satan's ongoing attempts to break our fellowship with Jesus and, as a result, greatly minimizes any impact by the enemy.

**There are times, however, when we must move beyond standing firm and engage the enemy in actual combat:**

- when we're taking significant steps of faith for spiritual growth,
- when we're invading enemy territory (through evangelism, for example),
- when we're exposing him for who he really is,
- when we repent and make a clean break with the world, a long-held sin pattern, or an unholy relationship,
- when God is preparing us, individually or corporately, for a great work for his glory.

1. The question: once you're wearing your spiritual armor and still find yourself bombarded by spiritual opposition, how do you engage in and win the battles?

2. The answer: Ephesians 6:16–17

    v. 16: "In addition to all, taking up the shield of faith with which you will be able to extinguish all the flaming arrows of the evil one."

    v. 17: "And take the helmet of salvation, and the sword of the Spirit, which is the word of God."

3. We can almost predict when the enemy will attack us.
    a. When we are growing spiritually.
    b. When we invade enemy territory.
    c. When we expose Satan for who he really is.
    d. When we repent and make a clean break with worldly or sinful patterns.
    e. When God is preparing us for a great work for his glory.

4. "Taking up the shield of faith."
    a. The metaphor explained: the shield was a large, layered piece of equipment that could link with others to protect an entire row of soldiers. Its layers could extinguish flaming arrows.
    b. Definition: *Faith* in this context is our absolute confidence in *God*, his *promises*, his *power*, and his *program* for our lives. Though rooted in the objective reality of the gospel and our new standing with God (justification) through Christ (saving faith), this faith refers to our "present faith in the Lord Jesus for victory over sin and the host of demonic forces."[5]
    c. Its purpose: to quench *all* the fiery missiles of the evil one.
    d. "Fiery darts/missiles": The schemes, temptations, lies, deceptions, and attacks aimed at God's people to get us to shift our trust to something or someone other than God. Examples include blasphemous thoughts, hateful thoughts, doubts, a burning desire to sin, unexplainable conflict with others, and waves of discouragement or depression—all often rooted in lies about God's identity or our new identity in Christ.

- Classic examples: Genesis 3; Matthew 4:1–11.
- Classic methodology: disguise, doubt cast on God and his Word or on you and your worthiness. Then provides appealing, immediate alternatives rooted in the pride of life, the lust of the eyes, or the lust of the flesh (1 John 2:15–16).

    e. Application: Darts of doubt and deception must be immediately met by the shield of faith (i.e., your active, present, application of truth to your personal situation as soon as you recognize a dart has been received). How?

- Trusting in God's character: God has my best in mind (Ps. 84:11; Rom. 8:32).
- Trusting in God's promises and Word: he will accomplish what concerns me (Num. 23:19; 2 Peter 1:2–4).
- Trusting in God's program and timing: his ways are not always easiest, but they are always best (Jer. 29:11).

5. "Take the helmet of salvation."
    a. The metaphor explained: A securely fastened helmet protects the head of the soldier and the mind of the believer.
    b. Definition: (1) Obvious allusion to the security we have as saved, justified believers, safe from Satan's attacks. But, the focus is on *present deliverance from sin*. (2) The helmet of salvation is the certainty of deliverance from sin and the protection of our minds in the battle.
    c. It's not something you can do. You receive it, but it's something you must allow God to do in your mind.
    d. How? Focus is God's renewing of the believer's mind (Rom. 8:5–8; 12:2). *2 Corinthians 10:5—The battle is for the mind!*
    e. Practically: prayer, worship, music, Scripture study, teaching, Scripture memory, fellowship.
    f. Paul calls the helmet our hope (certainty) of God's deliverance (1 Thess. 5:8).
    g. Application: Christians who are not filling their minds with Scripture are like warriors going out to battle without a helmet.

6. "Take . . . the sword of the Spirit."
    a. The metaphor explained: a light, two-foot sword was used in close, hand-to-hand combat. It required sharp mental and manual skills.

b. Definition: The sword of the Spirit is the Word (*rhema*: the spoken word or words given to us by the Spirit of God) to do close, hand-to-hand combat with the lies and deceptions of the enemy. The truth of God's Word quoted and applied to the specific lie or deception of the enemy will allow you to "take every thought captive to the obedience of Christ."
c. Application: Jesus models for us the use of the sword of the Spirit in Matthew 4:1–11.
  • Implications for us: Psalm 119:105; Psalm 119:9, 11.
  • Practical considerations: note that the sword is both a defensive and an offensive weapon (Heb. 4:12).

## Personal Application
*What You Need to Remember*

1. The prerequisite to engaging the enemy and winning is a healthy spiritual life.
2. Understand your position in Christ.
3. Discern when demonic influence may be the cause.
4. Claim God's promises out loud (1 John 4:4; 5:4–5).
5. Take your authority and position in Christ to command demonic forces to cease their activity and depart.

# 9

# When You're Attacked

Consider that the devil does not sleep, but seeks our ruin in a thousand ways.

Angela Merici

The first time it happened, I was lying in bed, half awake and half asleep. It started out like a bad dream, but suddenly there was a foreboding evil presence in the room. There was intense pressure on my chest that felt like a five-thousand-pound weight crushing me and a tightness around my neck that completely closed my windpipe. I was paralyzed; I couldn't move any part of my body except my eyes. I was desperate for air like someone under water who can't get to the surface fast enough. My thoughts were racing: "Oh, God, help me, help me, Jesus, help. . . ." I could see my wife asleep next to me, and I just kept praying and praying, clueless as to what was going on and wondering how in the world someone could suffocate in his own bed. And then the pressure suddenly left. I gasped for air, I could move again, and I sat up in bed, coughing, my body as soaked with perspiration as if I had played basketball for two hours. The hair on the back of my neck was sticking straight up, and there was a sense of manifest evil in the room that I had never felt in my life. I was scared to death. It was hostile, demonic activity, and this experience was repeated many, many times over the next few years.

That was in Santa Cruz, California, a community in which occult activity thrives, and it happened shortly after I had moved there to pastor the Santa Cruz Bible Church. I had experienced several spiritual attacks as a pastor before, but never one like this. This one required more than what we've discussed so far in the first two sections. This wasn't some subtle deception or lingering condemnation; this was an offensive frontal assault. And I didn't know what to do.

I don't tell that story to be dramatic, and neither do I tell it to portray myself as a strategic target of the enemy. I know it's not unique to me. In fact, almost every time I share that experience when I'm speaking, a few heads in the audience begin to nod as though they know exactly what I'm talking about. People come up to me afterward and say, "That happened to you? I thought it was just me and that I was going crazy." Although somewhat unusual, this experience seems to be fairly common to many who have been the object of frontal demonic attack.

What do you do when you experience an attack like that? This goes beyond the majority of spiritual warfare in which we will ever have to engage. This requires decisive, authoritative action against the enemy. And I—a seminary-educated pastor who knows quite a few Bible verses to quote—sat up in bed and thought: "I need to pray, and it needs to be out loud. But if I do that, my wife might wake up. And if she hears her husband, sweaty and breathing heavily, talking out loud in the middle of the night to someone she can't see, she's going to think I'm a nut case." The enemy loves to immobilize us with that kind of pride and fear, and one reason is because of what it did to me. I sat there motionless in the darkness of the night, filled with fear and anxiety, and unable to fight the fight for a painfully long time.

About two years after that first experience in the dark, a friend related a similar incident. My friend had come out of a nominally Christian background. He had attended church growing up and occasionally as an adult; he tried to be a decent guy, but he admitted that his life had never really demonstrated his salvation. He finally made a real commitment to Christ, and he began a process of discipleship. I invited him to join me every Sunday afternoon for the weekly basketball game in my driveway, and he came regularly over the next couple of years. I watched him prioritize his life, getting into the Bible, improving his marriage, ministering to others, and doing some pretty radical and generous things with his finances. He got off of the spiritual bench and became a high-impact player for the kingdom of God.

After playing ball one Sunday, he and I sat down for a talk as we frequently did, and he shared this story. "Something weird happened last night," he told me. "My wife and I were just sitting on the couch after the kids had gone to bed. It had been a great weekend, I felt really close to her, and I had my arm around her. We were watching some old movie, and she dozed off. It was a neat feeling, sitting there with my arm around my pretty wife and reflecting on all the ways God has blessed me. And then all of a sudden, a thought came out of nowhere. 'She's going to die. She's going to be taken away from you.' Within seconds I was totally convinced—and really scared. For reasons I can't explain, I was sure it was true. I didn't know when—whether it would be that night or sometime soon—but I just knew she was going to die. My body and emotions began to react as though a doctor had just told me my wife had terminal cancer and only had a few days to live. And then my mind went from there to questions: 'Why?' 'What kind of God would let that happen?' I wasn't sure I could believe in a God like that. Soon I was wondering whether God was really good, and I didn't know what to do. Chip," he said, "what was going on with all of that? It was completely illogical, with no basis whatsoever, and yet it was so real. I'm still struggling to shake some of those thoughts even today."

My answer? Spiritual warfare. God's voice may prepare people for tragedy sometimes, but not by bombarding them with fear and anxiety. My friend was immediately catapulted into deep doubts about God, so it was clear where the voice came from because the Holy Spirit never causes us to doubt God. Many people have had similar experiences, maybe with different manifestations, but with the same dynamics. This may be relatively rare compared to the kind of battle we've addressed so far, but it does happen. And when it does, will you know how to respond? The goal of Spiritual Warfare 301 is to equip you to deal effectively with this type of attack. So where do we begin? Let's review the truth we've learned about spiritual warfare before exploring how to engage the enemy during these frontal assaults.

## Four Facts You Need to Know

*Fact #1*: God has objectively defeated Satan and his agenda. He has delivered us from sin's penalty and power, and ultimately he will deliver us from sin's very presence. That's a fact. In the interim, we are involved in guerrilla warfare with demonic forces.

*Fact #2*: As believers, we have been transferred from the kingdom of darkness to the kingdom of light, and we have all the rights, privileges, and position that being a child of God entails.

*Fact #3*: The spiritual battle we fight involves a responsibility on our part to put on the spiritual protection God has provided for us. When we stand firm against the enemy, we can—and will—resist his attempts to deceive, accuse, and cast doubt. We do that by:

1. being honest with God, ourselves, and others as a prerequisite to all spiritual battle,
2. responding to the truth that God shows us about his will for our lives—righteous living,
3. clearly understanding and readily sharing the gospel message of grace.

*Fact #4*: The great majority of spiritual warfare need never go beyond the regular practice of living out our position in Christ by faith. Our practice of Paul's metaphor of the spiritual armor protects us from Satan's ongoing attempts to break our fellowship with Jesus and, as a result, greatly minimizes any impact by the enemy.

## Five Specific Times You Can Expect Spiritual Attack

There are times, however, when we must move beyond standing firm and engage the enemy in actual combat. These times aren't random. You can almost predict some of his attacks by becoming aware of what's going on in your life. There are at least five times when you might find yourself engaging the frontal assault from the enemy.

### 1. Spiritual Growth

First, Satan attacks us when we're taking significant steps of faith for spiritual growth. My friend, for example, was attacked with evil thoughts right after he had started memorizing Scripture. He was getting into the Bible on a regular basis, and he was also beginning to give generously of his finances to impact the world for Christ through our church and various other ministries. When he was growing up, his parents always gave him a dollar to put in the offering plate. As an adult, he figured about five bucks would do it—maybe twenty for those times when the service made him feel really good. Then he started writing some pretty substantial checks. "I don't just give them; I feel awesome about it," he told me. "It's like I can't believe I get to be a part of what God is doing through our church." And then he began sharing his faith. He was growing by leaps and bounds and investing his life in the kingdom of God. Guess what? He was ripe for attack. The enemy wanted to scare him back into mediocrity and ineffectiveness.

### 2. Invading Enemy Territory

A second time we may be attacked is when we're invading enemy territory. Getting involved in evangelism by sharing your faith, going on a mission trip, or reaching out to people in your community through your church is a threat to the enemy. Satan's desire is to magnify his harassment and obscure the blessings of being involved in fruitful ministry. If you're invading his territory, he wants to make you think it's not worth it.

For a clear picture of this dynamic, flip through the pages of the book of Acts. Almost every time Paul went to a new city to preach the gospel, a countermovement sprang up. And it was never a delayed reaction—or a casual one. The venom of the enemy was spewed out in multiple ways from multiple angles to try to get the witnesses of the gospel to stop their activities. Jewish legalists would beat them, stone them, stir up rumors about them, and otherwise try to harass them; pagan worshippers, sorcerers, and demons would start protests and encourage the masses to attack them as threats to the local business and culture; and physical hardships would not-so-coincidentally cluster around seasons of fruitful ministry. Imprisonment, shipwreck, flogging, and theft were not uncommon. And if none of that worked, dissension and deception would creep in and infiltrate the church later. (For a more comprehensive list of Paul's hardships, see 2 Corinthians 11:23–33. Paul doesn't imply in those verses that all of his difficulties were inspired by the enemy, but in other passages, he does attribute many of them to Satan's schemes.)

## 3. Exposing the Enemy

The third instance when Satan attacks directly is when we're exposing him for who he really is. I've taught these principles several times, and whenever I have—and I mean this reverentially and literally—all hell has broken loose. As you discuss these things with other Christians and people begin to get a glimpse of who this enemy really is, he plans retaliation. He wants it to stop. He doesn't want people to learn how he operates. He'll intimidate out in the open if he has to, but he's much more effective in secret. When you disrobe him and expose what demonic spirits are actually doing, you take some heavy-duty shots. To be honest, one of the reasons I was reluctant to write this book was the opposition and attacks that I knew would come my way and to those close to me. Every time I have taught this material, I have experienced multiple frontal and covert attacks from the enemy on my life, my marriage, my family, and my co-workers in ministry. In fact, while preparing this text, a co-worker who was helping me with the manuscript rattled off a list of obstacles and difficulties that were so overwhelming and noncoincidental that only our awareness of the source and his tactics could keep him from complete discouragement.

## 4. Breaking with the World

A fourth example of a high probability for attack is when we repent and make a clean break with the world, a long-held pattern of sin, or an unholy relationship. When couples who have been living together realize that they need to get right with God, suddenly there's spiritual opposition. I've seen it again and again. Our church had a ministry called "Celebrate Recovery" for recovering addicts. When someone came off of heroin, cocaine, or some sexual addiction, we would know that for the next three months, things were going to be terrible. Why? The enemy's work was being undone. He was losing one of his own.

This is extremely important to understand because so often when someone makes a clean break with the corruptions of the world, that person's expectation is that things will get better. We instinctively believe that righteousness and obedience make for a life of peace. I can't count the number of times I've talked with young men or women who had chosen to break off an unholy relationship, stopped living together, or walked away from an addiction and then were totally discouraged a week or two after that decisive step of obedience.

"I just don't understand it, Chip," they would tell me. "I did what was right—what God wanted me to do—but things aren't getting any better. In fact, they're getting worse." And they would share a story of a lost job, a conflict with a close friend, illness, depression, car wrecks, being robbed, or being ostracized by unsympathetic friends.

Sometimes we forget that we are in a spiritual battle for our souls. The battle is fierce and the implications are eternal. The enemy does not give up his strongholds in our lives easily or lightly, and to be ignorant of his schemes can prove disastrous.

## 5. Blessings to Come

A fifth occasion for attack is when God is preparing us individually or corporately for a great work for his glory. Spiritual opposition is often one of the things that lets you know that God is up to something good in your life or in the life of your church or ministry. It appears to us as a random attack, but citizens of the unseen world know much more clearly than we do how spiritual work is advancing. The attacks aren't out of the blue; they're strategic. One of my professors used to say that spiritual opposition was always a good sign. It meant that we were worthy of the attention of the kingdom of darkness.

It sounds counterintuitive, but this is a critical point to remember. Unexplained spiritual opposition can be an excellent indicator that God has something very special around the corner. In my own life, this has been a great comfort during times when the opposition was intense but I had little or no understanding of its cause.

My most recent experience was during my move from California to my new role as president of Walk Thru the Bible. The first eighteen months were some of the most difficult of my life. Within weeks of being directed by God to take this new assignment, everything bad that could happen did happen. The move was horrendous: the truck taking our cars was wrecked in an ice storm, the furniture came before the house was ready, the refrigerator was dropped and broken, my wife had two oral surgeries within the first few months in Atlanta, we had a death in the family, the economy bottomed out when the ministry needed funds, and the transition of merging two ministries into one was the most stressful experience I can ever remember.

The circumstances became so adverse and the pressure so overwhelming that I remember asking God, "Is this my reward for leaving a place I loved and following you in obedience?" I was discouraged, depressed, and whining. I honestly saw no human way to make it through all that was before us. And then God's still, small voice reminded me that sometimes his greatest blessings are preceded by the most fierce conflict. As an act of submission, but with little or no emotion, I promised the Lord that even though I did not understand what he was doing, I would nevertheless refuse to quit. It was an act of the will and a choice to believe that what God had spoken to me, he would fulfill. But my present circumstances and emotions were screaming just the opposite.

Looking back, I can see that God was up to something very special. The battle was being fought in heavenly places for the future of Walk Thru the Bible and Living on the Edge ministries. Who could have dreamed that our international ministry would double during this difficult time, that the radio ministry would expand to hundreds more stations and into ten additional countries, and that the synergy of the two ministries would multiply into eighty-five countries only a year after our most difficult days? Be on guard. Sometimes the worst of times are designed by the enemy to get you to give up on God's clear direction because he knows of the powerful and wondrous blessings that are ahead.

## Personal Application: What about You?

Don't let these things scare you. That's exactly what the adversary wants. The blessings of being used by God to impact the world always far outweigh the harassments of the enemy. You have to choose between fear and faith, and the latter is by far the better choice. The best response is to forge ahead with the knowledge of how to engage the enemy successfully.

We learned in Ephesians 6:10–12 that we are commanded to be strong in the Lord and to put on the full armor of God. Why? Because there's a struggle that is not against flesh and blood but is waged on an entirely different level. We battle against rulers, powers, and world forces of this darkness. We are to stand firm. Then in verse 13, we begin to learn *how* to stand firm. We take up the full armor of God, girding our loins with truth, putting on the breastplate of righteousness, and anchoring our feet in the gospel of peace.

Once we've done all that, we are to take up three more items. But these are not like the last three we looked at. Those were defensive—critical for holding our position. These next three have offensive implications. They are the necessary equipment we will need to go forward against the attack. The knowledge presented in the next three chapters will enable you to avoid wandering aimlessly in the spiritual battlefield. You will know how to engage the enemy with confidence. When you are wearing your spiritual armor, and still you are bombarded with spiritual opposition, there are specific strategies you can use to win—decisively.

### In Your Life

- Does the kind of frontal assault described in this chapter seem hard to believe? Why or why not?
- Have you ever been the victim of an intense spiritual attack? What was going on in your life at the time?
- When you read through the list of occasions when the enemy is likely to assault, does it frighten you? If so, how does that play into the hands of the enemy?

# 10

## Cultivate Invincible Faith

The ultimate cause of all spiritual depression is unbelief. For if it were not for unbelief, even the devil could do nothing. It is because we listen to the devil instead of listening to God that we go down before him and fall before his attacks.

Martyn Lloyd-Jones

It happened almost every week, but I had no idea what was going on. I would prepare all week to preach and get excited about how the message was coming together. Then the morning before our Saturday evening service, I would go out for a couple of hours to review my sermon. After praying through the major points and deciding on the illustrations to use, I couldn't wait to preach, because I sensed God had spoken to me and wanted me to share it. And then sometime between the enjoyable review of my notes and the actual delivery of the message, something unexplainable would happen: I would go through an inexplicably dark time right after lunch. I would get genuinely depressed, thinking thoughts like, "Man, I don't want to preach. I don't even want to be a pastor. I'm a terrible person." I experienced waves of condemnation that sapped all my motivation and energy. It was so bad that I was sometimes even reluctant to get in my car and drive to the church.

For me, that was new. I had always been a very upbeat and optimistic person. I always considered the glass more than half full. I'd get blue occasionally like everyone does when circumstances are discouraging, but I had no major issues with depression. Deep, dark nights of the soul were very rare for me. And now, sometimes in a matter of only thirty seconds, I would go from enjoying life to feeling like I was the worst husband, father, pastor—maybe even the worst person—in the world.

Finally I caught on to what was going on. It was happening about the same time every week, always only hours before I was to preach. It was bizarre and unrelated to the rest of my life. I could be feeling great, enjoying a Saturday with Theresa and the kids, but then I would fall into this dark, spiritual funk. I was under siege, and the attacks were piercing thoughts hurled at me with pinpoint accuracy. This pattern occurred over and over until I recognized it and learned some specific ways to use the shield of faith to quench the fiery darts of the enemy. I had to learn to trust the promises of God, reminding myself that if he called me to preach, he would give me the strength to do it. "God is not a man, that He should lie, nor a son of man, that He should repent" (Num. 23:19). If he promised that I could do all things through Christ who strengthens me (Phil. 4:13), he could be counted on to keep that promise. I had to learn to believe in specific verses and apply them to the weapons of the enemy.

### The Shield of Faith

At the time Paul wrote to the Ephesians, there were two kinds of shields. One was a small, round, handheld shield like the kind you always see in movies about ancient gladiators. That's not what Paul was referring to. The shield in this passage was about four feet high and two and a half feet wide. It had hooks on the sides to link it to other shields in a line so that an entire row of soldiers could advance without exposing themselves to incoming arrows. It was common for enemies to dip their arrows in pitch, light them, and then pelt the opposing soldiers with thousands of destructive, flaming missiles. So the Romans made their shields with iron and two layers of wood, wrapped them in linen, and covered it all with leather. But they would leave a gap between layers so flaming arrows could penetrate far enough into the shield to be quickly extinguished. One soldier is said to have come in from the battle lines with two hundred once-fiery arrows still stuck in his shield. That's the metaphor Paul uses, and his readers understood exactly what he meant.

This ability to quench arrows that have the potential not only to pierce but also to start a destructive fire is what faith does for us. Faith in this context means *absolute confidence* in God, his promises, his power, and his program for our lives. It is rooted in the objective reality of the gospel and our new standing with God—the saving faith that justifies us—but it is more specific here. This kind of faith refers to our present trust in Jesus for victory over sin and demonic hosts.[6] Its purpose is to quench all the fiery missiles hurled at us by the enemy. Claiming God's promises by faith, trusting in his unchanging character, and holding up his truth will deflect and extinguish all the enemy's lies. Regardless of the form which these incoming flames take, faith overcomes.

The fiery darts of the adversary are the schemes, temptations, lies, and attacks aimed at God's people. Their goal is to get us to shift our focus from God onto something or someone else. If the enemy can get us to be afraid, feel guilty or condemned, get discouraged, or lose hope, he can move our dependence away from God and onto something much less worthy.

*Blasphemous thoughts* are one type of dart. Sometimes people are shocked when I give this example, but I think it's pretty common. Have you ever been praying and having a really sweet time with God, and all of a sudden a vulgar word goes through your mind? God delivered me from cussing very soon after I became a Christian, but sometimes when I'm having a really good prayer time, my thoughts are interrupted by some crude word or phrase, and I wonder where in the world it came from. Then it's followed up by condemnation: "What kind of Christian are you that you could think something so despicable while communing with God?" That's the enemy shooting a flaming arrow at me, trying to intrude on a powerful activity that could hinder him from his agenda.

Another potential dart is *hateful thoughts*. We sometimes are consumed by anger or hatred toward someone else. Unresolved anger is one of the most common ways we unknowingly leave ourselves vulnerable to demonic attack (Eph. 4:26). We start making assumptions about that person's motives, and the more we think about it, the more he or she gets on our nerves and provokes in us a sense of vengeance.

*Doubts* are another kind of fiery missile—not just the little doubts with which we all struggle, but even big-picture doubts about the gospel itself. We wonder whether we're saved or whether God even exists. Those are the kind of thoughts that scare us, and we don't even feel we can express them to other people because they just wouldn't understand. They might question our status as a true believer for even entertaining such thoughts.

I shared in an earlier chapter a time of intense spiritual opposition while ministering in India just days after a tsunami hit. The battle was a bombardment of doubts like I have not encountered since the first two years after my conversion. And they weren't small doubts or partial doubts about a verse here and there. They were gargantuan doubts about God himself, about the reliability and validity of the Bible, and about Jesus as the only way and provision for mankind. The idols, the poverty, the darkness, and the overwhelming devastation of the tsunami, combined with my extreme fatigue, gave the enemy a prime opportunity to seek to derail my life at the foundation.

I share this because I believe I am not alone. When our minds are attacked by illogical, unbiblical, and deceitful lies that are so heretical we are too ashamed to disclose them, they are not brought into the light and often cause us to stumble. Fortunately for me, my co-worker had exactly the same experience at the same time, and we were able to see through the deception.

Sometimes we suddenly have *a burning desire to sin*. Everything in us wants to do something we know is wrong, and we're confronted with a golden opportunity to give in to the urge. Sometimes a relationship that we've had for years suddenly erodes into *unexplainable conflict*. Maybe a thought flashes through our mind and we question the other person's motives. "I wonder if he's telling the truth. I wonder if he's been honest with me all these years." Despite years of a good track record, we have doubts about a close friend's loyalty and integrity. We've already mentioned the sudden onslaught of *overwhelming times of depression*—not depression from a chemical imbalance, lack of sleep, or normal grief, but times when you're in the sunlight one minute and then, as if someone flipped a switch, you're in the pits and you don't want to come out. These are just a few examples; you can probably think of many, many more. All of them are flaming darts. This is how the enemy works.

## Seeds of Doubt

If you want to know exactly how Satan undermines faith, Genesis 3 and Matthew 4:1–11 are great places to start: the temptation of Eve and the temptation of Jesus. Study these classic examples of the enemy's methodology carefully, and you'll see a pattern. It often begins with a disguise. You don't know where the deception comes from, but somehow it casts doubt either on God and his Word or you and your worthiness. Both with Eve and with Jesus, Satan began by suggesting that the verdict is still out on God's truth. "Has God said, 'You shall not eat from any tree of the garden'?" asked the serpent in Genesis 3:1. "*If* You are the Son of God, . . ." he said to Jesus in the wilderness (Matt. 4:3, italics added). He does the same with us. "Is that really what God meant by that promise? How could a good God have let that happen?" Satan doesn't really care how he gets us there, but he wants us to think that God is cruel, indifferent, harsh, unloving (at least toward us), or a stern taskmaster. The first step is to question God's identity as we understand it.

Satan's second step is to cause us to focus on our own identity or worth. "You will be like God, knowing good from evil," he told Eve (Gen. 3:5). He promised all the kingdoms of the world to Jesus in exchange for his worship (Matt. 4:8–9). He fills us with pride over our own rights and identity, or he fills us with questions of our worthiness. "You call yourself a mother?" "You think you're a real man?" "You're terrible. You have no business pretending you're a Christian." As long as he can get us to think inaccurately about God, ourselves, or others, he can take us down a dangerous trail.

Having created a window of opportunity, Satan then offers an appealing, immediate alternative rooted in the three broad sins outlined in 1 John 2:15–16: the lust of the flesh, the lust of the eyes, and the pride of life. I believe every temptation in Scripture falls into one of those categories. The flaming missiles will exploit or appeal to your flesh, your eyes, or your ego. If his questions have made us vulnerable through doubt, he has found an opening in the shield of faith, and he'll aim right for it in one of those three areas.

The only effective response is to believe what God has said. When we sense the darts of doubt and deception, we raise the shield of faith, which can extinguish everything the enemy flings at us. We apply the specific truth of God's Word to our personal situation as soon as we're aware of an incoming missile. We don't evaluate our situation by visible circumstances, moods, or suspicions. We insist on God's truth regardless of any other message we're receiving, and we trust it implicitly.

## Strengthening Faith

Let me give you three specific examples of how faith can remain strong when attacked. The first is an example of *trusting in God's character* and the fact that he always has our best in mind. Remember the friend I told you about in the last chapter? He had just started to get things right in his relationship with God and with others, and he had a sudden, overwhelming fear that his wife was going to die. A lot of parents have had similar thoughts about their children, sometimes in the middle of the night or in a dream. The emotions can be so real that you begin to function and make decisions on the basis of fear, and you begin to question God's goodness. I told my friend that he had to take the truth of God's Word and hold it up. Psalm 84:11, for example, says, "The Lord God is a sun and shield; the Lord gives grace and glory; no good thing does He withhold from those who walk uprightly." Romans 8:32 says the same thing in a different way: "He who did not spare His own Son, but delivered Him over for us all, how will He not also with Him freely give us all things." I reminded my friend that God is on his side, that he is compassionate and loving, and that he is eager to be our friend. The root of the word *goodness*, used so often to describe God, is a word that means "generosity." As Tozer says, God "takes holy pleasure in the happiness of his children."[7] He wells up with joy when good things happen in our lives, and Satan's darts try to keep us from knowing and believing God's feelings for us. If we hold up the shield of faith by trusting in God's character, we can extinguish the flames of that arrow.

A second example is the one that began this chapter. I considered it an extraordinary honor to preach God's Word, and I would get excited about it every week. But hours before the first service each Saturday, my will and my energy to preach were frequently suppressed with a spiritual malaise. When we are shrouded in gloom for no apparent reason like that, *trusting in God's promises* and his Word will dispel the darkness. Numbers 23:19 tells us that God does not lie or fail to keep a promise. The assurance of 2 Peter 1:2–4 is that God has granted us "precious and magnificent promises" so we can participate in his divine nature. Once I saw the pattern of sudden, unexplained, spiritual opposition occur every Saturday afternoon, I did two things. First, I began to quote God's truth out loud, claiming his promises as true over and above my emotional perception. Second, I shared my burden with a few friends who began to pray for me weekly at the time these episodes normally occurred.

More recently, there have been times at Walk Thru the Bible when I was so discouraged about the transitions we were making and what a sagging economy was doing to our finances that I just dreaded going to the office. I would have to remind myself—and quote out loud—that God would supply all our needs according to his riches in glory (Phil. 4:19). I asserted these truths about God's provision for my situation, reminding myself that God's Word cannot be violated, and the enemy would soon disappear. The malaise or the dread would vanish, and I would be able to get on with the work God had called me to do.

A third example is about *trusting in God's program and timing*. God's ways are not always easiest, but they are always best. Jeremiah 29:11 is a classic passage: "'I know the plans that I have for you,' declares the LORD, 'plans for welfare and not for calamity to give you a future and a hope.'" When a dart flies into your life saying, "You don't really need to pay that person back," you can cling to the truth that God's program for integrity is best in the long run. When a dart says, "One little peek won't hurt," you can hold up God's plan for purity, even when it's hard. When a dart says, "Get out of this marriage," you can step back and say, "No, God has a plan for marriage. It's a tough season, and everything in me wants to opt out, but Lord, I trust you and I will keep my commitment to you. I know people who have been married for decades, and all of them say there were times when they felt like bailing out, but now they are glad they didn't. Love is not a feeling; it's giving someone what he or she needs most when it is least deserved. That's how God loved me, and I choose to stick with the program."

God gives us his views on numerous issues, so you don't need to let the enemy's missiles drive you beyond God's boundaries. You claim his promise and hold it up in faith against a specific missile coming at you. But I warn you, this is a real battle. Everything in you will want to quit, withdraw, bail out, cross the line, forfeit, and give in. As you hold up the shield of faith, though, verbally affirming God's truth and his promises against every dart, you will extinguish them one by one. This is not general guesswork; there's nothing vague about it. It is taking God's Word and promises as they apply to particular situations at particular times.

**Personal Application: What about You?**

Darts of doubt and deception must be immediately met by faith. The shield extinguishes every flaming arrow of the enemy when you actively apply truth to your situation. It is essential to trust in God's character, in his promises and Word, and in his program and timing as soon as you recognize an incoming missile. Flaming arrows are deadly and precise. The only way to render them ineffective is to plant your shield of faith firmly on the ground and kneel behind it, letting the blazing points of the aggressor vanish in the depths of your shield of faith and be snuffed out.

**In Your Life**

- Think of a flaming dart that has pierced your life in the past. Which of God's promises could have spared you from the wound you received?
- Which kind of faith does the shield most represent—the faith that saves us or the faith that applies God's Word to specific situations daily?
- Why is it hard to believe God's promises? In what ways do we try to place conditions on them or water them down?
- What are three specific situations to which you need to apply faith today? Which promises of God would it be appropriate to trust in these situations? (Some good starting points are listed below.)

| Area of Temptation | Promise |
|---|---|
| Temptation to sin | 1 Corinthians 10:13 |
| Financial needs | Philippians 4:19 |
| Strength and endurance | Philippians 4:13 |
| Adverse circumstances | James 1:2–4 |
| Uncertain future | Psalm 84:11 |
| Fear | Isaiah 41:10 |
| Anxiety | Philippians 4:6–7 |
| Personal crisis | Psalm 23 |

# 11

# The Battle for Your Mind

The spiritual battle, the loss of victory, is always in the
thought-world.

Francis Schaeffer

You could see the evidence of worry on his face. Years and years of anxiety were written into each wrinkle, the graying eyebrows, the sagging corners of his eyes, and even his pale coloring. He had been a faithful Christian from early in his life—church every Sunday, almost-regular Bible readings, consistent tithes, service as a deacon, and no hint of moral failure. He had been married for decades and raised a couple of respectable children, and he had run his business honestly. He was a fine, upstanding citizen with an awful lot of stress.

His stress had compelled him to live his life extremely conservatively. In his business, that made for moderate success. As a Christian, that made for mediocrity. He dismissed opportunities for extravagant steps of faith. They were always too risky—something an unstable person would do. Besides, he said, you could never know if God was really leading you or not. He also dismissed opportunities for extravagant generosity. He never gave more than a tithe because "one never knows when one might need something for a rainy day." He rarely expressed any emotion—to anyone, really, but especially in his worship to God. He may have loved others, but no one could tell; he never let his love show itself. That would have required too much vulnerability. Though he had never made any major mistakes—not the kind people can see, anyway—he was full of regrets. His sins were relatively few, but he had no hope of putting them behind him; he was only human, after all. He did know a few Bible verses about forgiveness, but only the really important ones—John 3:16, of course, and his favorite: "You will know the truth, and the truth will set you free" (John 8:32 NIV). Except he looked like the truth had made him miserable. He did everything that people expect a good Christian to do, and he did it with painful persistence.

What was this man's problem? He was eaten up with doubts, anxieties, a lack of confidence in God's power, and a fear of the unknown. And to him, almost everything was unknown. He was certain that he wanted to be a Christian, but he was uncertain about everything else. He believed the Bible is the Word of God, but he was too suspicious of his understanding to ever stand firmly on it. He took steps forward in his Christian walk, but they had to be small and predictable steps. He could never bring himself to believe God's extravagant promises. Any voice that urged him to cast all his cares on his Father came across to him as the voice of irresponsibility—and wishful thinking. He gave what was necessary of his time, talents, and treasure, but he never gave out of any kind of passion. Passion, in fact, had to be subdued; it's hard to be filled with doubts and enthusiasm at the same time. Uncertainty won't allow for that sort of nonsense—not in worship, not in service, not in relationships, not in work, not in anything. When it came down to it, this man wasn't even sure of his own salvation. To him, the gospel was only a reasonably safe bet. His thinking may have made him a solid citizen, but he was a miserable Christian. He had lost the battle for his mind long ago. And it was written all over his face.

There's an answer for someone in that kind of bondage to his own distorted thinking. In fact, it's more than an answer. It's an effective antidote to worry, discouragement, doubt, despair, and even boredom. It applies when we are tempted to embrace relativism, another religion, a watering down of the gospel, or any other such tactic that corrupts our understanding. It won't guarantee that we will never fail, but it will guarantee that failure isn't final. Underneath all the uncertainties of life is a rock-solid foundation, and the only way we can stand on it is in the way we think. Our thoughts have far more influence on us than our circumstances or our relationships do. If a redeemed mind truly understands salvation and is set on the Spirit of God himself, it will lead to fruitfulness and victory. And it will have to be protected very, very well.

## "Take the Helmet of Salvation"

The last piece of armor a soldier would put on was his helmet. It was made of bronze and leather, and its importance was obvious: if you're hit on the head, you're out. So immediately before going into battle, an attendant would bring a soldier his helmet and help him fasten it securely.

There's an obvious allusion in this metaphor to the security we have in our salvation, our new birth when we were justified by grace through faith and delivered from the kingdom of darkness. But the focus in this verse is on our present deliverance from sin. There are many senses of salvation in the Bible—from enemies, from sin, and from captivity, for example—and three tenses of salvation in the New Testament: we have been saved ("justification" as described in Rom. 8:24; Eph. 2:8), we are being saved ("sanctification" as described in 1 Cor. 1:18), and we will be saved ("glorification" as described in 1 Cor. 3:15; 1 Peter 1:5). We're used to hearing about salvation in the past tense—the moment we come to Christ. That's when we are freed from sin's penalty and its power in our lives is broken. But the word itself literally means "deliverance," and it is, more often than not, used to mean salvation from a threatening enemy (you can find numerous examples in the Psalms). We can live in the confidence that God is accomplishing victory for us *today*. We can experience deliverance on a daily basis.

The helmet of salvation, then, is the certainty of deliverance from sin and the protection of our minds in battle. The helmet of salvation may be seen as the ability to reason logically and wisely from a biblical worldview, no matter how that worldview comes under attack. It is not something we can do for ourselves. We must choose to receive it, but the passive voice in this verse implies that only God can make it happen.

To see how that works, look at Romans 12:2—the same truth from a different angle. The mind is again the focus. In this verse, Paul instructs his readers not to be conformed to this world but to be transformed by the renewing of their minds. The verbs are in the same passive voice—"do not [allow yourself to] be conformed," but "[allow yourself to] be transformed." We allow it and participate in it, but God actively does it in us with our cooperation. It's his work.

Why is God so concerned about our minds? According to Scripture, that's where the battle is. Many Christians believe the invisible war is primarily about their circumstances, their behavior, their work, or their relationships. It's true that all of those things are relevant, but none of them is the priority. We noted earlier that most of the battle is in our thought life—that's where Satan can manipulate people toward his ends discreetly and invisibly. If he can distort our thoughts, our emotions, and our knowledge, then our behaviors and relationships will fall the way he wants them to. And even if he doesn't manage to turn us to overt evil, a little bit of distorted thinking can neutralize us and render us practically ineffective, as with the man at the beginning of this chapter. Human

133

thinking is ground zero in this war, and if we haven't been diligent to fill our minds with God's truth and operate out of what he teaches us, we lose. The helmet of salvation guards the most influential organ in the invisible war.

That's why God is so concerned about our minds, and it's also why Satan is so concerned about them. They are a threat to him, and verse after verse emphasizes how critical protection is in this area. An obvious example is 2 Corinthians 10:3–5. It describes the weapons of our warfare as spiritual, not physical, and then applies them directly to "speculations and every lofty thing raised up against the knowledge of God." The goal is to take "every *thought* captive to the obedience of Christ." When Jesus prayed his last, lengthy prayer before the Father, he asked that his disciples would be prepared and protected—primarily in their knowledge of the truth. "Sanctify them by the truth," he prayed, and the next line made it absolutely clear what he was talking about: "Your word is truth" (John 17:17). Romans 8:6–7 also gives us a clear picture of the critical role of the mind: "The mind set on the flesh is death, but the mind set on the Spirit is life and peace, because the mind set on the flesh is hostile toward God." And as we saw earlier, the "god of this world" is able to thwart nonbelievers from accepting the truth. How? He has blinded their *minds* (2 Cor. 4:4).

### A New Testament Command: Renew Your Mind

The New Testament's emphasis on the human mind can be seen on almost every page, from instruction about what is true, to warnings against the deceptions of false teachers, to the role of our thinking in our spiritual transformation, and on and on. So putting the helmet of salvation on is not a matter of getting a little extra protection; it can't be done with a quick morning prayer, and it can't be approached casually. It's the difference between eternal truth and fatal error, even between life and death itself. That's why we need a helmet. It is imperative that we keep God's Word in our mind and Satan's lies out of it.

Here's how that plays out. You may go through all sorts of doubts and struggles, bombarded with the flaming missiles of the enemy. The shield of faith will extinguish them, but faith can only function around the truths you've been taught. You can't have specific faith in principles you don't know (or remember). Your mind needs to be filled with foundational knowledge, like the fact that you have been justified and your eternity is secure, or the understanding that you are God's child and have kingdom authority over the adversary. Regardless of what you go through, you have a hope that will never fade. The promises of God are certain—all of them are "yes" in Christ Jesus—because God always comes through. A believer who knows these things and clings to them will not only survive and not only stand firm in a crisis, but he or she will thrive in it. A believer who does not know such things will be easily diverted and distracted, often to the point of complete ineffectiveness.

We can know and reflect on that truth when our days are casual and our lives are running along pretty smoothly. But can we default to that truth when we're in the midst of a crisis or attack? That's when we need it most. In order to have it when it is most needed, we have to incorporate it into every area of our lives. The knowledge of our deliverance—past, present, and future, with an emphasis on the present—should fill our prayers, our worship, our music, our Bible studies, our Scripture memory, our teaching, and our fellowship. When we're filled up with real knowledge of God and his truth, there's not much room for any counterfeits.

Paul used this metaphor again in 1 Thessalonians 5:8, where believers are told to put on "the hope of salvation" as a helmet. These eternal truths of salvation, faith, and hope flow from a mind that has allowed itself to be saturated in God's Word, cultivated in faith and dependence, and transformed by the Spirit. In the cosmic conflict, the front lines are between your ears.

## The Battle for My Mind

My first year at Walk Thru the Bible was probably as difficult a time as I've ever had in my personal life. It was definitely the most difficult time I've ever seen my wife go through. A lot happened around the time of our move from Santa Cruz to Atlanta—the death of her mother, leaving a home and a church we loved, and all the uncertainty of a new kind of ministry in a new place. I've never seen her so discouraged. When you wake up in the middle of the night and you hear sobbing in the pillow next to you, you know times are tough. We men like to fix things, and this was something I just couldn't fix.

That was at home. Then I would go to work and realize that although I had already learned to trust God for hundreds of thousands of dollars as a pastor of a church, that wouldn't be enough. As the leader of an international ministry, I now had to learn to trust him for millions of dollars. That's hard to do when the economy is heading south, as it was then, and especially hard in a ministry that is going through a transition from leadership by its founder to leadership by someone completely new to the organization.

I cried out to God every day, and some days I just cried. I knew about dry seasons, but this felt like a drought of biblical proportions. I didn't know if my wife was going to make it through this season, I didn't know if the organization was going to make it, and I didn't even know if I was going to make it. I poured out my complaints to God: "You promised me. You told me this is what you wanted me to do. Either I didn't hear your voice, or I'm the dumbest guy in the world. I loved that church in Santa Cruz. Why did I do this?" Though I had already made a decision never to go there in my thinking, the darts of doubt and discouragement kept coming and coming. I wished I could get inside my wife's heart and fix all the loss and hurt she had just been through. I wished I knew some billionaire donors just itching to fund some of our projects. But I was practically helpless. I couldn't fix anything. I knew this was going to be a journey—a hard one.

Then one day the thought came to me. "Okay, Chip. What if your wife doesn't make it? What if Walk Thru the Bible goes down the tubes? What if *Living on the Edge* has to go off the airwaves? What if everything you've ever worked for turns to ashes? Do you remember that if you die tomorrow, you'll be with your Father forever and ever and ever?" The truth of salvation as it applied to this situation started to sink in. I realized that the worst that could ever happen to me would end in glory.

In my heart of hearts, I knew my motives for moving to Atlanta to lead Walk Thru the Bible were pure. Even if I had been deluded, I did exactly what I thought God wanted me to do. I had left security and gotten out of my comfort zone to follow him. If it all blew up in my face and ended in utter disaster, I would still be with God one day. And he would know that there was at least one son in California who said, "I want to believe you to the point of stepping out and taking a radical risk, and I know you honor love and faith." God could use some other organization to reach the world, develop another ministry, and work something out with my wife. But my ultimate hope couldn't be in those things. I had to understand that the worst thing that could ever happen to me was that I could die.

Think about that. It seems a bit morbid on the surface, but if you are a child of God, you have a final, secure, and unchanging hope that no circumstance, person, or tragedy can take from you. It doesn't matter if you're going bankrupt, one of your children has cancer, your business partner has bailed, and your finances are in the ditch—whatever. From a human perspective, the worst that can happen to someone who is a believer is death, and the moment you die, you're with Jesus. What's so bad about that? Being with Jesus in a perfect environment forever and ever, with all of your longings and desires fulfilled in him? Ultimate hope puts everything else in the perspective of eternity. *That's* the helmet of salvation.

God miraculously came through on all of those things I was so worried about. As is the case with most of the things we obsessively worry about, my worst-case scenarios never came to pass. My wife is fine (God even relocated two sons and their families to be near us), Walk Thru the Bible's finances took a turn for the better, and we experienced exponential growth beyond my wildest dreams. I'm not crying every other day, and I didn't die—not yet. But even if none of my current plans and dreams worked out—if I fell flat on my face and failed—it wouldn't be ultimate. Salvation guarantees it. That helmet protects me from all my dread of failure and loss, even when the threats come from the destructive plans of a powerful enemy.

That's how Paul could be so seemingly reckless with his life. He followed hard after God's lead, no matter how many dangers it took him into. When he said he had already given himself the sentence of death (2 Cor. 1:9), he was really saying, "I've got the helmet of salvation on." It's hard to hurt someone who is already dead, isn't it? The enemy, circumstances, or other people can threaten all they want, but if we can say, "I'm already dead. Go ahead and shoot me. I'll just go to be with Jesus," we're secure. And we're able to take enormous steps of faith when God prompts us to do so.

The helmet of salvation gives us an unquenchable hope. Our hope is not in finances, in people, in circumstances, or in all our desires coming through for us. Our hope is in the person of Christ. The psalmist had the right perspective: "Whom have I in heaven but You? And besides You, I desire nothing on earth" (Ps. 73:25). That's what salvation is ultimately about, and it will keep you sane and at peace. When the darts come flying in, put up the shield. And then whatever you do, keep the helmet of salvation strapped on tightly.

## Personal Application: What about You?

Christians who are not filling their minds with Scripture are like warriors going out to battle without a helmet. A raging battlefield is a frightening place to be when your head is exposed. Just ask any veteran who saw combat in any war of any period in history. The head is the body part of a soldier that is the most guarded—and the most targeted.

Your shield of faith will become dramatically more efficient in quenching the enemy's flaming missiles if you give faith a lot to hang onto. The way to do that is to saturate yourself in the salvation God has given and continues to give freely, not just for your soul and spirit, but for your body, your work, your relationships, your service, your finances—everything. Let your mind be immersed in such truths and absorb them as deeply as you can. Then when you find yourself in the middle of a battle, you will know beyond the shadow of a doubt exactly where you stand.

## In Your Life

- Why is God so concerned about your mind? Why is Satan so concerned about it?
- Think of what you consider to be your biggest failure or mistake in life. How does the helmet of salvation protect you from ongoing guilt and regret—or from fear about "the next time"?
- Can you identify any patterns that undermine your faith and confidence in God's ability to deliver? What verses can you use to counter them?
- Think of two or three people you know who have borne much fruit in God's kingdom. How would you describe their faith? Do they take any risks in their walk with God? Do they more often seem defeated or encouraged? What do their characteristics tell you about their helmet of salvation?
- What changes does your mind need to make in order to walk confidently in the knowledge of present deliverance and salvation?
- What game plan do you need to put into practice in order to fill your mind with the truth?
- What do you think your life would look like if you considered yourself already "dead" and lived only for God and his glory?

## Resources for Putting on the Helmet of Salvation

*Daily Walk Bible*—Read through the Bible in a year with helpful commentary and application so you can understand it for yourself (www.walkthru.org).

*Overcoming the Pain of Your Past* (audio series)—Exposition of Ephesians 1–3 to learn your identity in Christ and how to think about God, yourself, and others (www.lote.org).

*The Miracle of Life Change* (book, DVD, and audio series)—Exposition of Ephesians 4 to learn how to practically live out your new identity in Christ in everyday life (www.lote.org).

*The One Year Walk with God Devotional: Wisdom from the Bible to Renew Your Mind*—Daily readings to transform your thinking (www.walkthru.org).

# 12

# Wield Your Weapons

The deceit, the lie of the devil, consists of this: that he wishes
to make man believe that he can live without God's word.

Dietrich Bonhoeffer

In Santa Cruz, there's a strip called Pacific Avenue. It's a popular place
to walk, with a lot of things to see and do. There are several bars in the
area, and they are usually filled at night.

I remember walking down Pacific Avenue one evening, about the
time of night when it would normally begin to get a little rowdy. I saw a
couple of very tall, massive guys in tight T-shirts standing on the sidewalk
outside one of the bars. These guys were agitated about something, but
they were not the type you wanted to mess with; they looked mean and
pumped up on steroids. They were drunk, out of control, and bigger
than the bouncer who was trying to deal with them—and who apparently had just called the police. I didn't want to get too close, for obvious reasons, but I was curious enough to stay and see what happened.
(What can I say? I'm human.) So I stood at a distance to see how the
situation would play out.

In a couple of minutes, a police car pulled up to the curb with its
lights flashing. The door flung open, and out stepped an officer who
was ready to take charge—a female officer who was no taller than four-
foot-eleven! I felt sorry for the bouncer; he was probably hoping for a
six-five weightlifting officer, not a four-eleven woman. This was going
to get ugly. Or so I thought.

I could not have been more wrong. This diminutive yet confident officer walked briskly up to the troublemakers and said, "Gentlemen, do we have a problem here?" The guys started trash-talking, and she immediately interrupted. "Excuse me," she said as she pointed to her badge. "I'm authorized by Santa Cruz County to enforce the law. I'd like both of you over against the car right now. Do you understand?" They balked. Then she put her hand on her revolver, and I've never seen two burly drunk guys get sober so fast. They got up against the car, spread out their legs, put their arms behind their backs, and the situation was under control.

Why on earth did two enormous bullies submit to a very small woman? In any other situation, that confrontation could have been disastrous. But this situation had nothing to do with size and strength. The police officer had authority, and the guys on steroids didn't. *And* she had the reinforcements of the government and a .45 pistol to back her up. Her position enabled her to say, "You must do what I say. And if there's any problem with that, I have a powerful weapon at my side that I can and *will* use to enforce it immediately."

## "Take the Sword of the Spirit"

A Roman soldier had an "enforcer" too. It was the sword he always had with him. This wasn't a long, heavy sword; it was a light, two-foot weapon used in close, hand-to-hand combat. It had to be easily accessible and ready to use—and the soldier had to be very proficient in using it. The sword was the only strategic weapon that could be used when the enemy was close, so warriors spent hours upon hours with it in their hands, working on their dexterity, getting used to the feel, and letting it become second nature, as familiar as their own limbs. Their lives depended on their diligence in keeping their skills honed and ready for battle at any moment.

Paul defines the Christian's sword for us in Ephesians 6:17: it is the Word of God. Most times in New Testament Greek, *word* is a translation of *logos*. Not here. In this case, it's a translation of *rhema*—the specific, spoken word (or words) given to us by the Spirit of God to do close, hand-to-hand combat with the lies and deceptions of the enemy. God applies his Word (*rhema*) by making the Word (*logos*) alive and active in our specific situations. It comes to us so we can take every thought captive to the obedience of Christ. The difference between the *logos* and the *rhema* is the difference between a stockpile of weapons and a sword in a highly skilled hand. One is the invaluable arsenal; the other is a specific, well-timed deployment. The *rhema* is the sword of the Spirit.

The fact that the Word of God is the sword *of the Spirit* teaches us two important truths. The first is that we must be in a vital relationship with the Spirit of God in order for this weapon to be operative. The Spirit is "command central." One rogue soldier wielding a sword independently of the rest of the battalion is not going to be very effective. Just the opposite, in fact; he will be, for all practical purposes, asking for immediate defeat. Though the armor and the weapons of God are very useful in your personal life, there is a bigger picture. Paul is writing to a church, not an individual. The agenda is God's, and the strategy is to fit an overall mission. Your personal issues are important to God and likely fit with the larger mission, but he expects the sword to be more than personal. It is a tool of the kingdom. The degree to which your life is filled with the Spirit of God and fits with the kingdom of God is the degree to which your swordplay will be effective.

The second truth, which flows out of the first, is that this is not a weapon we may use any way we want to. It is made alive only by a power beyond ourselves. We are the ones who fight with it, but a stronger hand enables it. If we begin to depend on our own authority in using the Word and not the Authority behind the Word, we become like a power-abusing cop—in love with the immediate result rather than the higher agenda (see Luke 10:17–20 for a warning from Jesus about this tendency). All authority we have is imparted to us—given by grace. We are not the masters of demons; we are fully endowed ambassadors of the Master of all. With this in view, let's look at how we are to practically use the sword of the Spirit in our battles with the enemy.

## The Perfect Example

If you want to learn how the *rhema* really works, look at Jesus. He clearly modeled this with a very straightforward example for us to follow. Matthew 4 relates how Jesus was tempted at the end of his forty-day fast in the wilderness. Satan came to him and said, "If you are the Son of God, command that these stones become bread." Jesus's response was piercing: "*It is written*, man shall not live on bread alone, but on every word [*rhema*] that proceeds from the mouth of God" (vv. 3–4, italics added). Then the adversary proceeded to round out the temptation in every area: the lust of the flesh, the lust of the eyes, and the pride of life. Every time, Jesus answered with, "*It is written; it is written; it is written.*" He was quoting the *logos* of God, but he was battling with the *rhema* of God—the *logos* applied to his specific situation. When he was done, Satan departed.

That's what it means to resist the devil. You resist him by putting on the full armor of God, standing firm, taking the sword of the Spirit, and wielding that powerful weapon against all the deception. You counter lies with truth, and truth wins every time.

Are you beginning to get an idea of how serious studying and meditating on Scripture and renewing your mind are? This is not a matter of squeezing in that brief, daily devotional with a chapter of Bible reading, and then thinking, "Okay, check. I've done that. No need to feel guilty now." This is the substance of life. Psalm 119:105 says that God's Word is a lamp to our feet and a light to our path. Moses told the children of Israel that they were to take to heart every word he commanded them. For this word "is your *life*" (Deut. 32:47, italics added). "How can a young man keep his way pure? By keeping it according to Your word. . . . Your word I have treasured in my heart, that I may not sin against You" (Ps. 119:9, 11). Over and over again we get a clear, biblical picture that God's Word is a life-and-death matter. Like a sword in the hand of a soldier, it needs to become second nature.

If you are going to have the full armor of God in this invisible war, you will have to be a man or woman of the Book. There's no way around it. That's not a legalistic requirement any more than daily nutrition is; it's just a necessity of life. You need to read the Bible in such a way that you can think your way through key chapters, you can recall core passages that you've memorized, and your mind is renewed so that you can know who you are and where you stand in Christ. You need to be able to reach into your arsenal—Jesus picked his weapons straight out of Deuteronomy—and pull out a sharp and decisive point to refute the enemy. That defeats him, and he will leave.

Practically, it helps to picture the Word as it is portrayed in Hebrews 4:12: "For the word of God is living and active and sharper than any two-edged sword, and piercing as far as the division of soul and spirit, of both joints and marrow, and able to judge the thoughts and intentions of the heart." The way to keep the armor on is to be in God's Word with a humble, open heart, so that as you read it, God can reveal where your heart is and restore you. You should never be in a position of having to wield a sword that is a weapon only. This sword is to be a part of you so that when you fight, you are expressing the power of the Word that has already done its work in you.

142

### How It Works in Our Lives

Let's go back to my bedroom for a minute. Do you remember the story I told at the beginning of chapter 9? In the middle of the night I felt an oppressive evil in the room and was paralyzed for some period of time until God answered and I could move and breathe again. We left off at the point when I sat up in bed, dripping with sweat and scared to death. What did I do? I got hold of myself and realized that this was demonic. (It wasn't all that difficult to figure out, with my heart beating out of my chest and my neck hairs standing at attention.) Then I realized my position in Christ: "Greater is He who is in you than he who is in the world" (1 John 4:4). Then I quoted—out loud—1 John 5:4–5: "Whatever is born of God overcomes the world; and this is the victory that has overcome the world—our faith. Who is the one who overcomes the world, but he who believes that Jesus is the Son of God?" Then I quoted out loud Revelation 12:11: "They overcame him [Satan] by the blood of the Lamb and by the word of their testimony, and they did not love their lives to the death" (NKJV). And finally, I did something I didn't have any substantial experience doing. I said: "Evil and demonic spirits, I come against you now in the name of the Lord Jesus. I am a child of God, I am covered by Jesus's blood, and I command you right now in Jesus's name to leave my house and to leave me alone." And the evil presence was gone. The demonic spirits obeyed my words just like the two drunks obeyed the petite, female police officer. They obeyed because I did not come in my own strength or power; I came with official authority derived from God and with a lot more than a .45 pistol—the spoken, all-powerful, living Word of God. To be honest, though, I have to tell you that on a few subsequent occasions when this sort of thing happened, it took as many as four or five times of extended prayer before relief came. It was sometimes a prolonged battle. But when relief did come, it was usually immediate.

A lot of times people will hear a story like that and think, "Well that's in a weird place like Santa Cruz. I've heard about that in occult centers and mission fields, but you don't expect a regular person like me to have to deal with that, right? You have to go to seminary or something for that kind of training, don't you?" And my answer is emphatically "no." This is normal Christianity all over the world. As I mentioned earlier, I've rarely shared this experience without people coming up afterward and telling me that it has happened to them in almost the same way. It is a very common way for demonic forces to scare God's people, especially when those forces feel threatened.

When Satan attacks—and don't assume it won't happen to you—remember that four-foot-eleven police officer who powerfully subdued two massive bullies on the street one night. Your size and strength are not the issue, but your position and your weapon are. You have to know how to exercise your authority, and you have to know your weapon well enough to use it effectively against the enemy. If you do not know God's Word well enough to quote it, and if you aren't certain of your position in Christ, you are like an unarmed officer who left his badge at home. The results can be disastrous.

### Personal Application: What about You?

You are a child of the King of Kings and the Lord of Lords. Your badge is your position in Christ, and you have on your side the sword of the Spirit, which is the Word of God. Whether they like it or not, dark powers must believe, respond to, and obey the authority of every child of God who wields the Word of God against specific issues. Luke 10:19 is a promise given to all believers: "Behold, I have given you authority . . . over all the power of the enemy, and nothing will injure you." Authority trumps power, even all the power of the enemy. You don't have to be strong, super-spiritual, or seminary-educated. You do, however, have to claim who you are and act on what is true. You also have to know the Word well enough that the possibility of your using it won't be considered an empty threat. Study the Word, be ready in and out of season, and act decisively when attacked.

### In Your Life

- Have you ever experienced an incident that you knew the enemy was behind? If so, how did you respond? How did the enemy respond?
- Intellectually, do you understand that your grasp of the Word of God is more important than the amount of food and sleep you get? Practically, does your life reflect that truth?
- If someone were to evaluate how well you have mastered your weapon—the Word of God—what would the evaluation say?
- What steps can you take to sharpen your skills with your sword? (It is important to write this answer out in the form of a plan and then stick to it.)
- Think about the illustration of the petite police officer who subdued two enormous drunks. Is there anything in your life that would prevent you from functioning with the same confidence and authority demonstrated by the officer?

**Resources to Wield Your Weapon Better**

*Explore the Book* (audio series)—How to read, study, and get a grasp of the Old and New Testaments, by Chip Ingram (www.lote.org).

*Authentic Worship* (series)—An exposition of Romans 12 for living out our faith day by day, by Chip Ingram (www.lote.org).

## What You Need to Remember

If you were a rookie cop, you would need to review the steps of how to handle a crisis situation. Consider this a summary of your training manual, and make it your guide to a clear response to the evil one:

- As a prerequisite, maintain a healthy spiritual life.
- Understand your position in Christ as spelled out in the first three chapters of Ephesians.
- Discern when demonic influence may be the cause.
- Claim God's promises out loud.
- Then take your authority and position in Christ, and command the demonic forces to cease their activity and depart.

It's that simple—not easy, but simple. When you do that, Satan will leave. Evil has to bow to the *rhema* of God.

# Spiritual Warfare 401

## Deliverance from Demonic Influence

Prayer is that mightiest of all weapons that created natures can wield.

Martin Luther

With all prayer and petition pray at all times in the Spirit, and with this in view, be on the alert with all perseverance and petition for all the saints, and pray on my behalf, that utterance may be given to me in the opening of my mouth, to make known with boldness the mystery of the gospel, for which I am an ambassador in chains; that in proclaiming it I may speak boldly, as I ought to speak.

Ephesians 6:18–20

## Introduction: Special Forces

1. We are in an invisible war—Ephesians 6:10–12.
2. We are to prepare ourselves for battle—Ephesians 6:13–15.
3. When we resist the enemy, he will flee from us—Ephesians 6:16–17; James 4:7.
4. Intercessory prayer is pivotal and essential for corporate and individual deliverance—Ephesians 6:18–20.

Summary: The means by which believers are to withstand and overcome the attacks of the enemy in spiritual warfare is by *consistent*, *intense*, and *strategic* prayer for one another in conjunction with the personal application of the armor of God.

## Executive Summary

*Chapters 13–15*

1. Intercessory prayer is our most powerful and strategic corporate weapon in spiritual warfare.
   a. Prayer has a direct impact on spiritual warfare (Mark 9:29).
   b. Prayer provides/assists in the deliverance of others who are undergoing spiritual attack (Luke 22:31–32).
   c. Power falls where prayer prevails (Acts 1:14; 2:42; 3:1; 4:31; 6:4; 10:9). Church history is replete with examples.

2. What kind of prayer brings God's deliverance and power in the midst of spiritual attack?
   a. Consistent prayer (Eph. 6:18a).
      - "with all prayer and petition" = all kinds of prayer
      - "pray at all times" = prayer on all occasions
      - "pray in the Spirit" = in communion with and directed by the agency and power of the Holy Spirit
   b. Intense prayer (Eph. 6:18b).
      - "be on the alert" = literally: without sleep, vigilant
      - "with all perseverance" = enduring, not giving up
   c. Strategic prayer (Eph. 6:18c–20).
      - "for all the saints" = that God's messengers will be bold
      - "utterance may be given" = that God's message will be clear and have opportunity
   d. Summary: The *missing ingredient* in most Christians' lives and in most churches is the commitment and regular practice of intercessory prayer. Scripture indicates that consistent, intense, and strategic intercessory prayer—both individual and corporate—will in fact deliver us from the evil one.

   The great people of the earth today are the people who pray. I do not mean people who talk about prayer; nor those who say they believe in prayer; nor yet those who can explain about prayer; but I mean those people who take time and pray. They have not time. It must be taken from something else. This something else is important. Very important, and pressing, but still less important and less pressing than prayer.[8]

   S. D. Gordon

3. The ministry of deliverance.
   The great majority of teaching in the Bible has to do with alertness, preparation, defense, and being proactive to prevent demonic

influence from breaking our fellowship with Christ or thwarting God's program for our lives. *What are we to do, however, when the enemy gets a foothold in our lives or in the life of someone we know and love?*

a. Its validity

- Jesus regularly exercised this ministry (Mark 1:23–27, 39).
- The apostles regularly exercised this ministry (Luke 10:1–20).
- The early church regularly exercised this ministry (Acts 8:9–13; 13:8–11; 16:16–18).
  —Justin Martyr (ca. 100–165)
  —Tertullian (ca. 160–225)
  —Origen (ca. 185–254)
  —Athanasius (ca. 296–373)
- The New Testament writers provide clear direction concerning this ministry (James 4:1–10).
- Contemporary, balanced deliverance ministries do exist and help many people.

b. Its problems

- Extremism and fanaticism tend to negatively color this ministry.
- Confusion concerning demon possession versus oppression of believers clouds this ministry's validity among Christians.
- Fear and ignorance have caused many to simply ignore this ministry.
- Those who engage in this ministry are often tempted by pride or become so singularly focused they fall into theological error.
- Assigning blame for all one's problems to demonic influence versus assuming personal responsibility and using biblical common sense call this ministry into question.

c. The causes of demonic influence

- Active seeking
- Yielding to sin: John 8:34
- Spiritual rebellion: 1 Samuel 15:23
- Participating in the occult: Deuteronomy 18:10–11 (divination, sorcery, omens, witchcraft, spells, and attempting to contact the dead)
- Association with those involved in satanic activity: 2 Corinthians 6:14–16
- Unresolved anger and bitterness: Ephesians 4:26–27

d. New Testament evidences of demonic influence
- Severe sickness: Matthew 12:22
- Divination (telling the future): Acts 16:16
- Unusual physical strength: Mark 5:2–3
- Fits of rage: Mark 5:4
- Split personality: Mark 5:6–7
- Resistance to spiritual help: Mark 5:7
- Other voices from within: Mark 5:9
- Occult powers: Deuteronomy 18:10–11

e. The cure for demonic influence
- General purpose
  —Victory is through the cross of Christ (Col. 2:15).
  —Victory is in the name of Christ (Matt. 10:1; Acts 5:16).
  —Victory is by the power of the Holy Spirit (1 John 4:4).
- Specific steps for deliverance from demonic influence
  —Accept Christ (John 1:12).
  —Confess sins (1 John 1:9).
  —Renounce the works of the devil (2 Cor. 4:2).
  —Destroy occult objects (Acts 19:17–20; see also 2 Chron. 14:2–5; 23:17).
  —Break friendship with occultists (2 Cor. 6:14–16).
  —Rest in Christ's deliverance (Col. 1:13).
  —Resist the devil (James 4:7).
  —Meditate on and apply the Word of God (Matt. 4:4, 7, 10; Eph. 6:17).
  —Engage in corporate prayer (Matt. 18:19).
  —If necessary, perform exorcism in the name of Christ (Acts 16:16–18) by a spiritually mature counselor (Gal. 5:16; Eph. 5:18) who maintains humility (James 4:7), wears spiritual armor (Eph. 6:12–17), knows the Word of God (Matt. 4:4, 7, 10), and is supported by prayers of believers (Matt. 18:19; Eph. 6:18).

f. Additional resources for help when you suspect demonic influences:

*The Adversary,* Mark I. Bubeck

*Overcoming the Adversary,* Mark I. Bubeck

*Powers of Evil: A Biblical Study of Satan and Demons,* Sydney H. T. Page

## Personal Application
*What You Need to Remember*

There are several steps you can take to bring your life into conformity with Scripture on the matter of prayer and deliverance.

1. Assess the quantity and quality of your prayer life. Is it everything both you and God want it to be? If not,
   a. At the beginning of your normal prayer time, make two requests of God: "Today, lay on my heart the issues that you want me to pray for until you are ready for me to stop," and, "In the next few days, impress upon me how my prayer life should change from what it is now."
   b. Then be sensitive to the ways in which God might be leading you. Ask for his guidance until you are convinced you have received it.
2. Pray through the ACTS model (Adoration, Confession, Thanksgiving, Supplication) to make sure your prayers are well-rounded.
3. Ask God to make you spiritually sensitive to demonic influence and to give you wisdom as you seek to discover your role in a specific need for deliverance.

Be persistent in these prayers. God wants you to understand this subject as much as you do—actually, more than you do. Pray earnestly and constantly for the understanding he wants you to have.

# 13

# The Missing Ingredient of Your Life

> We must not confide in the armor of God, but in the God of this armor, because all our weapons are only mighty through God.
>
> William Gurnall

The missionary was serving as a medic in Africa. Periodically, he had to travel by bicycle through the jungle to a nearby city for supplies. It was a two-day trip, so he would camp in the jungle overnight. He had always made the trip without incident, but one day when he arrived in the city he saw two men fighting. One was seriously hurt, so he treated the man, shared Christ with him, and went on his way.

The next time the missionary traveled to the city, the man he had treated approached him. "I know you carry money and medicine," the man said to the missionary. "Some friends and I followed you into the jungle that night after you treated me, knowing you'd have to sleep in the jungle alone. We waited for you to go to sleep, planning to kill you and take your money and drugs. As we started to move into the campsite, we saw twenty-six armed guards surrounding you. There were only six of us, so we knew we couldn't possibly get near, and we left."

When he heard this, the missionary laughed. "That's impossible. I assure you, I was alone in the campsite." But the young man pressed the point. "No, sir. I wasn't the only one who saw the guards. My friends saw them too, and we all counted them."

Several months later, the missionary attended his home church in Michigan and told of his experience. A man in the congregation interrupted his presentation by jumping to his feet and saying something that left everyone in the church stunned. With a firm voice, he said, "We were with you in spirit!" The missionary looked perplexed. The man continued. "On that night in Africa it was morning here. I stopped by the church to get some materials for a ministry trip. But as I was putting my bags in my trunk, I felt the Lord leading me to pray for you. It was an extremely strong urge, so I got on the phone and gathered some other men to come to church and pray for you." Then the man turned to the rest of the congregation. "Will all of those men who prayed with me that day stand up right now?" And one by one they stood up—all twenty-six of them.

That's a fascinating story reported by a reputable periodical, and I have no reason to question its authenticity. But you may wonder what it has to do with spiritual warfare and deliverance from demonic oppression. I believe it has *everything* to do with deliverance and the invisible war. It is a great illustration of the missing ingredient in the lives and churches of many of us.

We've gone through the basics: we're in an invisible war, a struggle that is not against flesh and blood. We moved from there to an explanation of how we can prepare ourselves for battle by putting on the full armor of God and standing firm. Then we examined the weapons we have for resisting the enemy when standing firm isn't enough—those times when we have to engage our adversary in actual combat. The final element of our warfare is the greatest—and most neglected—weapon we have. Intercessory prayer is pivotal and essential for corporate and individual deliverance.

The grammar in Ephesians 6 is very instructive. There is no break between verses 17 and 18. If I were to adjust the punctuation of this verse—that's okay to do, since the Greek text has no punctuation in it—it would look like this: "Take the helmet of salvation and the sword of the Spirit (which is the word of God) with all prayer and petition. Pray at all times in the Spirit." In the context of putting on the armor of God, Paul moves right into prayer and petition without taking a breath. We are to wear our armor with all kinds of prayer at all times in the Spirit. Specifically, Paul asks for prayer that he would open his mouth with boldness to proclaim the mystery of the gospel. The weapons of our warfare and prayer are integrally connected.

I firmly believe that the missing ingredient in most Christians' lives and in most churches is prayer. I mean strong, biblical prayer—the kind Paul writes of in this passage. It's the kind of prayer that is full of faith and trust, and as we'll see, it's consistent, it's intense, and it's strategic. It brings change in churches and in lives. Bondage is broken, old habits are discarded, people become courageous, walls between believers are broken down, and relationships are restored. God uses this kind of prayer in conjunction with the armor of God to transform lives.

Do you want to pray like that? Do you want to see God change your life and your church, to bring friends and relatives to Christ? The battle doesn't go away—you still have to put on the armor, take up the sword of the Spirit, and hold up the shield of faith—but when you wage the battle with this kind of prayer in communion with the Holy Spirit, God does supernatural things. I may not understand exactly how it works; there are a lot of things about the sovereignty of God and the free will of human beings that I don't understand. But the Bible doesn't tell us to be able to explain his commandments before we follow them. It does tell us, over and over again, to pray biblically, strategically, intensely, and powerfully in a way that prompts radical change.

## Intercessory Prayer

Intercessory prayer is our most powerful and strategic corporate weapon in spiritual warfare. It is the necessary means by which we as believers are able to withstand and overcome the attacks of the enemy. If that sounds like an overstatement, maybe it will help to take a look at some biblical examples.

Jesus said that prayer has a direct impact on spiritual warfare. In Mark 9:14–29, the disciples were attempting to cast out a demon, but it wasn't working very well. They came to Jesus and asked him what the problem was. "This kind cannot come out by anything but prayer," he told them (v. 29). Apparently there are evil spirits that are not compelled to respond by any other means. Jesus also once told Peter that Satan had asked to sift him like wheat. "But I have prayed for you," Jesus told him (Luke 22:31–32). Prayer assists in the deliverance of people who are undergoing spiritual attack.

The early church also knew the power of prayer. When Jesus had ascended and they were waiting for further instructions, what did they do? Acts 1:14 says they "were continually devoting themselves to *prayer*" (italics added). That's also what they were doing when Pentecost occurred, according to Acts 2:42: "They were continually devoting themselves . . . to *prayer*" (italics added). Right before the first major miracle of the church, Peter and John were going to the temple to *pray* (Acts 3:1). The first time persecution was leveled against the church, Peter and John returned from their flogging with an explanation of the privilege of suffering in Jesus's name, and then the believers who were gathered around them *prayed*. The room shook, the Holy Spirit came upon them, and they all began to speak with even greater boldness (Acts 4:31). The first dissension in the church came when some of the people were being neglected. So the apostles decided to appoint deacons to oversee the distribution of food. Why? So they could devote themselves to teaching and to *prayer* (Acts 6:4). When Peter saw a vision that would change his ministry forever, he was on a roof *praying* (Acts 10:9). If you go through the rest of Acts, you'll find the same pattern. Whenever God's supernatural power is evident by signs, wonders, transformed lives, and open doors that no one can explain, I can guarantee you that somewhere, someone has been praying. Power falls where prayer prevails.

### What Kind of Prayer Brings God's Deliverance and Power?

Often church members will declare that they want their church to be "a New Testament church." I understand that desire; it's my desire too. But do we really understand what that means? A New Testament church is a praying church. Not just a church that has prayer meetings, not a church that has a few prayer warriors behind it, but a church that is in the regular practice of coming together with urgent and intense prayer. Most Christians can say that their church is a praying church, but few can say they have seen supernatural power and progress running rampant in their fellowship. That's because Acts-type ministry doesn't happen from any old kind of prayer. A little prayer here and there when it's convenient is not what Paul is writing about in Ephesians. There is a specific kind of prayer that brings those kinds of results. It has three characteristics that come straight out of Ephesians 6:18–20.

### Consistent Prayer

The kind of prayer that brings supernatural results and deliverance is characterized by consistency. Verse 18 starts off with "all prayer and petition." The word for "all" is a general word for "all kinds," and the word for "petition" implies very specific requests. Sometimes we get stuck in one kind of prayer or another, but Paul is urging a diverse prayer life. ACTS is the best acronym I know that helps me get out of "monotone" praying:

- A for adoration: our prayers should be saturated with giving praise, honor, and glory to God.
- C for confession: let honest and open confession characterize your communication with God and others.
- T for thanksgiving: look in the rearview mirror frequently and thank God for what he has done.
- S for supplication: on behalf of yourself and others, boldly ask God for specific things for now and the future.

Anyone who prays through the ACTS acronym regularly will have a well-rounded, consistent prayer life.

"Pray at all times" (v. 18) means to pray on all occasions. While it is important to have set times of extended prayer—like the psalmist who writes that he will pray to God in the morning, at noon, and in the evening (Ps. 55:17)—the rest of life is to be punctuated with prayer as well. Informal, spontaneous times of prayer grow out of deep seasons with God. We can pray as we drive, in the middle of a conversation, when an ambulance rushes by, and when we're quiet and not really thinking about anything—until a vivid image of a need comes to mind. The kind of prayer God answers is consistent.

In the story at the beginning of this chapter, a regular guy was just putting some things in his trunk when God prompted him to pray for a missionary. Nearly everyone has had an impression like that on occasion, but what do we do with it? "Lord, please help so-and-so." I can just hear the Holy Spirit saying, "No, no, no. A little prayer isn't going to cut it. Gather some men of the church." The man in the story made a few phone calls one morning, and twenty-six people showed up. That doesn't happen in most churches I know. But when they came together, got on their knees, and prayed in communion with the Spirit, something miraculous happened. The burden led to a spontaneous response because the people in that church had cultivated a consistent prayer life.

A godly pastor in Atlanta took me under his wing during my transition from Santa Cruz to Atlanta and frequently coached me through some of my struggles. Some time later, I got an email from him: "Dear Chip, in prayer this morning, deeply prompted with a sense of urgency. I have no idea what's going on in your life. Took you before the throne." It could not have been more timely. I was dealing with several heavy issues and teaching on spiritual warfare at the time. His awareness of the Spirit reminded me that God knew exactly what was going on—and that God cared. That kind of awareness comes only through consistency.

## Intense Prayer

It is not enough to be consistent; our prayer also has to be intense. Paul says to "be on the alert" (v. 18), which literally means to be without sleep. Prayer should be a matter of vigilance, not a matter of going through the motions. Running through a list of people to pray for while trying to keep your mind from wandering is not what Ephesians refers to. This is the kind of prayer in which you are "on," you are focused and alert. And not only are you alert, but you're praying "with all perseverance." You endure and do not give up.

Sometimes when I pray, I'll start to wonder after about ten minutes if there's a ceiling on my prayers. It feels like I'm not getting anywhere. There have been occasions when I've thought, "This is just too hard, Lord. I'll see you later." You can probably relate; most Christians have had moments like that. It is important—absolutely essential—to break through that ceiling. You will probably never experience more opposition than when you pray consistently and intensely under God's leading. Demonic forces come to attention when people get into God's Word, but they have a greater fear than Bible study. They shudder when God's people begin to pray. There are reasons that prayer doesn't always come easily for us; we have enemies who want to make it difficult. We have to break through the barriers.

One of my heroes is Elisabeth Elliot, and I love what she wrote about prayer:

> People who ski, I suppose, are people who happen to like skiing, who have time for skiing, who can afford to ski, and who are good at skiing. Recently I found that I often treat prayer as though it were a sport like skiing—something you do if you like it, something you do in your spare time, something you do if you can afford the trouble, something you do if you're good at it. . . .
>
> But prayer isn't a sport. It's work. Prayer is no game. . . . Prayer is the opposite of leisure. It's something to be engaged in, not indulged in. It's a job you give priority to. It's performing when you have energy left for nothing else. "Pray when you feel like praying," somebody has said. "Pray when you don't feel like praying. Pray until you do feel like praying." If we pray only at our leisure—that is, at our own convenience—can we be true disciples? Jesus said, "Anyone who wants to follow me must put aside his own desires and conveniences" (Luke 9:23, TLB).
>
> In the wrestling of a Christian in prayer, "our fight is not against any physical enemy: it is against organizations and powers that are spiritual. We are up against the unseen power that controls this dark world, and spiritual agents from the very headquarters of evil" (Ephesians 6:12, Phillips). Seldom do we consider the nature of our opponent, and that is to his advantage. When we do recognize him for who he is, however, we have

an inkling as to why prayer is never easy. It's the weapon that the unseen power dreads most, and if he can get us to treat it as casually as we treat a pair of skis or a tennis racquet, he can keep his hold.[9]

## Strategic Prayer

At the end of Ephesians 6:18, Paul begins to put prayer in focus. First, he tells the Ephesians to pray for all the saints; then, they are to pray for him as God's messenger (v. 19). The point is for believers to be able to endure, to stand firm, and to be strengthened, and for the gospel to be proclaimed boldly and clearly.

We often get into our own little worlds when we pray, focusing only on our families, churches, finances, struggles—everything that specifically has to do with our own sphere of interest. Those things are certainly of interest to God; we *should* pray for them. But a lot of times what we are really asking is for God to arrange our lives in a way that would be easier, more comfortable, and more fulfilling. We are commanded to get past that and pray that the message might go out around the world—and that we would be bold in getting it out.

In verses 19 and 20, the word *bold* is used twice. The early church was characterized not only by prayer but by *bold* prayer. They were winsome and loving, but they were not afraid to be politically incorrect. They were bold because they knew the risen Lord, and that knowledge fueled intense prayers. They asked God for big things, and they asked him for strategic things: that their communities would be taken for Christ, that their churches would be unified, that their leaders would be empowered. If we follow their example, we will be diligently and persistently asking God to bless our pastors, to empower all of his servants, to spread the gospel throughout America and the world, and to make us bold and unafraid. There's a big difference between praying, "Lord, please help me find a parking place at the mall," and praying, "Lord, send me into your world unafraid and unashamed to declare your goodness and grace through Jesus." Our prayers should major on the latter.

"Prayer is the energy that enables the Christian soldier to wear the armor and to wield the sword," says Warren Wiersbe.[10] Scripture indicates that consistent, intense, and strategic prayer will deliver us from the evil one. If you've ever wondered what you're missing in the Christian life, look here first. A commitment to intercessory prayer changes lives.

Do you want to know who the most influential people in the world are? When we think of power, we usually think first about presidents and business moguls or cultural icons like movie stars and sports figures. But in God's economy, those people have very little influence. S. D.

Gordon words it well: "The great people of the earth today are people who pray. I do not mean people who talk about prayer; nor those who say they believe in prayer; nor yet those who can explain about prayer; but I mean those people who take time and pray. They have not time. It must be taken from something else. This something else is important. Very important, and pressing, but still less important and less pressing than prayer."[11]

## Personal Application: What about You?

What we've learned in Ephesians 6 is that our greatest success in spiritual warfare is when we understand that there is an invisible war, that God has given us armor to protect ourselves, and that as we walk in fellowship with him, the majority of the conflict is handled. We have also learned that during times of radical growth, effective advances in ministry, or any other activity that threatens the enemy, missiles will come flying toward us. But even then, we have the protection and the offensive weapons that we need.

What we need to remember—and this is what Paul was leading up to with his metaphor of the spiritual armor—is that prayer is powerful. In fact, it is probably much more powerful than you and I have ever imagined. The reason we aren't convinced of that fact is that we usually fail to pray consistently, intensely, and strategically. The enemy has done a good job of convincing us that prayer is a hit-or-miss attempt to get God to do what we want and that it is only effective on select occasions. Satan has spent a lot of effort on that sort of propaganda because he knows that prayer defeats him—always. Our casual attitudes about prayer are the result of his desperate and aggressive attempts to neutralize the most powerful weapon against him.

Knowing that, what will you do now? If you are content with the status quo in your effectiveness as a Christian, do what you have been doing all along. The same practices will reap the same results. But if you want to have a dynamic impact for the kingdom of light and against the kingdom of darkness, the answer should be clear. Pray. Pray with consistency, pray intensely, and pray with a plan.

## In Your Life

- Has your mind ever wandered during prayer? Do you get distracted? Do you feel that your prayers aren't getting past the ceiling? How often do these tendencies characterize your prayer life?

- Have you ever considered that your prayers are difficult because someone is opposing you in prayer?
- What are some steps you can take to "break through" in prayer?
- What kinds of requests do you usually bring to God? Do they fall more in the category of personal desires or kingdom purposes?
- What practical things can you do to help your church be a New Testament church when it comes to prayer?

DELIVERANCE
in a balanced ministr
- How much too
- Know of any?

N
O

# 14

## When the Enemy Gets In

---

We, calling on the name of Christ crucified, chase away all the demons you fear as gods.

St. Antony of Egypt

Our two Sunday night services were drawing quite a crowd, both in numbers and in diversity. They were geared toward young singles, and our leaders were very creative in reaching out to people from all kinds of backgrounds. The services were having a great impact, especially with those steeped in postmodern culture. I didn't teach in those meetings, but one night I had to pick up something from my office. I pulled into the parking lot just as the service was about to begin, and it was packed. As I got out of my car, I saw three people coming toward the building. At first glance, I had to remind myself that it wasn't Halloween. These three visitors were dressed completely in black with long capes, their hair was dyed in various colors, and they looked like their faces had been covered in whitewash. They had black circles painted around their eyes and their mouths. And they were coming to church.

It's an amazing thing to see three vampire-looking characters among the hundreds of people streaming into church. I heard later that these visitors became significantly disruptive. They sat in the back, and when the gospel was being preached, they prayed against the service and all things Christian. A number of people had to come and pray for them—and against them. They were steeped in the occult, driven by dark powers, and even possessed by their evil lords.

w that's an alarming example of people who have given themselves
er to spirits of the underworld. They have literally invited demons to
possess and control them. Deliverance for them is available if they will
repent and seek it, though it takes nothing short of an exorcism. But
this example is extreme. Most of our churches don't regularly encounter
such folks. What we do encounter, however, are demonic influences at
much more subtle levels. In terms of degree, the kinds of demonization
we encounter are seldom more extreme than the kind that visited our
church that Sunday night. But in terms of deception, the subtle kinds are
in some ways more dangerous. They are harder to see. Sometimes we
live with them much longer before we realize what we're dealing with.

As Christians, we never want the adversary to break our fellowship
with Jesus or to derail God's program for our lives. We want whatever
God has for us in all of its fullness, without wondering at the end of our
lives what we've missed out on. That's what this book has been about:
living in unbroken fellowship with God without being victimized by the
enemy's distractions and defeats. What we've covered to this point will
be helpful in preparing for the battle, in defending ourselves, in being
proactive to prevent demonic influence, and in thwarting the enemy's
frontal assaults. We now know how to keep him from getting in.

But what if he's already in? What if we've put up the shield too late? If
the enemy has already run rampant within the walls of our lives, shutting
the gates may seem pointless. If you or someone you know has given
Satan too much ground, much of what we've discussed so far may have
stirred up a lot of regrets without offering any real solutions. Disease
prevention doesn't help much when the disease has already done its dam-
age. What are we to do when the enemy has a foothold in our lives?

It would not be appropriate to discuss spiritual warfare without considering the issue of deliverance. There is so much confusion and even
controversy over deliverance ministries that some people avoid the idea
altogether. But there's a balanced, biblical way to approach deliverance
that doesn't require you to get a special degree or go off on a wild extreme.
I'm not an expert on this kind of ministry, but I do know what the Bible
says about it, and I've seen it operate effectively in the church. I believe
there are some specific tools that regular Christians can use to be a part
of deliverance when demonic oppression is evident.

## Deliverance Ministry: Its Validity

The first question most Christians have about a ministry of deliverance
is whether it's valid—especially whether it's valid for today. If one of the
defining characteristics of being a Christian is being like Christ, then it

would seem obvious that deliverance *is* valid for us today. Jesus regularly exercised this ministry. Mark 1:23–27 and 1:39 are two examples among many. I mentioned earlier that roughly 25 percent of Jesus's ministry had to do with deliverance and demonic oppression. That's a huge portion for something many people consider irrelevant today. I don't believe Jesus would have focused so much on deliverance if it were not valid.

"Well, that's Jesus. He's the Son of God," some might argue. But the apostles exercised this ministry as well, not just occasionally, but often. Jesus gave them authority to do so in Luke 10:19, and they used it many times afterward. It also can't be argued that this was a privilege of apostles but not of "regular" believers. The early church was very familiar with deliverance. From Simon the magician in Acts 8:9–13, to Elymas the magician in Acts 13:8–11, to the fortune-telling slave girl in Acts 16:16–18, deliverance is scattered all through the works of early believers. Apparently it was a big problem; new believers in Ephesus who had once been involved in demonic practices brought their occult objects to be burned in the center of town (Acts 19:19). No one in the church considered that spooky or "out there." It was normal practice, and it remained normal throughout the first four centuries of the church. We can find references to it from Justin Martyr (ca. 100–156), Tertullian (ca. 160–225), Origen (ca. 185–254), and Athanasius (ca. 296–373)—none of whom can be considered out of the mainstream of church history by any means. Deliverance is an important part of church history.

In Santa Cruz, we came into contact with people who identified themselves as witches or Satan worshippers. One summer a group of workers with Campus Crusade for Christ came to help our church and others in the area. After the service one night, they described to me their day of evangelizing in the community. They had met several people dressed completely in black—avowed Satan worshippers—who lived up in the hills and were very upset about the growth of the churches in Santa Cruz. These people told the Campus Crusade workers that our impact would not be long-lasting because they prayed regularly to demonic spirits to crush what was happening. What really alarmed our workers was that the people in black mentioned me by name and said they had been casting spells that would ruin both the church as a whole and me individually. Our summer visitors came away from the discussion convinced that demonic influences were thriving in the hearts and minds of certain Santa Cruz residents.

How would you respond to that? What if one of those spiritual captives came to you for help? Would you explain that deliverance was a New Testament phenomenon that no longer applies today? Surely God still has an answer for those caught in the web of the enemy's lies.

The New Testament writers provided clear direction for this ministry. They expected deliverance to be a part of Christian life. James 4:1–10, for example, gives a full set of instructions: submit to God and resist the devil, and the devil will flee. Draw near to God and he will draw near to you. Cleanse your hands, purify your hearts, humble yourself before God, and he will give grace. This is presented as a routine procedure in response to demonic influence and harassment.

Contemporary, balanced deliverance ministries do exist and help many people. There is a wide variety of opinions on this subject, and while I wouldn't necessarily agree with everything written by these authors, books by people like Mark Bubeck and Neil Anderson offer a generally balanced treatment with real-life examples from all over the world.[12] There are clearly times when demonic influence makes such inroads into a person's life that deliverance has to occur, and there are people and ministries that know how to do that.

## Deliverance Ministry: Its Problems

To be honest, though, there are a lot of problems with the practice of deliverance. For one thing, extremism and fanaticism tend to negatively color this side of ministry. You've probably seen examples on television—people who are going to stomp out the devil with all sorts of antics. I didn't grow up as a believer, and I would see that sort of thing on TV and think those people were nuts. Becoming a Christian didn't change my opinion of some of them. We live in a generation that so identifies deliverance with the extremes they see on TV or hear on the radio that the ministry is dismissed altogether.

Another problem is confusion over demon possession. Is there a difference between possession and oppression? Can a believer be possessed? Someone's answers to those questions determine to a large extent whether he or she believes deliverance is worthy of our attention. But the fact of the matter is that the New Testament never even uses the words *possession* or *oppression* with regard to demons. It uses a verb: "to be demonized." Later we'll discuss the extremes of demonization—all the way from simple opposition to complete control of an individual—but the idea that believers can't be touched by the devil at all is not what Scripture teaches.

Some Christians ignore this ministry out of fear or ignorance. When I speak on this subject, I usually have a long line of people coming up to me afterward expressing relief that their experiences weren't abnormal—hallucinations or the beginning stages of insanity. These are average, middle-of-the-road people, not people dressed in black with multiple body piercings who look like they just emerged from the underworld. I find that a lot of people in my audiences had thought they were unusual, and they were therefore afraid to talk about demonic encounters. They didn't want their spouses, friends, or anyone else to think they were crazy.

Another problem common to deliverance is the tendency of those who engage in the ministry to be tempted by pride or to become so singularly focused on it that they fall into theological error. They can be really sincere people, but if they've been involved in that ministry for a long time, they may perceive every toothache or flat tire as an attack of the enemy. They forget the part of the equation that says we live in a fallen world and bad things happen. If the wind blows hard enough, trees fall on top of houses and cost us a lot of money. If we're exposed to a virus, we have a good chance of becoming sick. These things happen. And as people created with free will, there's also the matter of personal responsibility. We all make choices, and sometimes our choices have negative consequences. That's not demonic. Satan isn't behind everything. He certainly energizes sinful flesh and infiltrates the systems of this world to control them, so we fall victim to all sorts of temptations and trials. But it's a fallen world, and sometimes we simply reap the results of fallenness.

Assigning blame for all our problems to demonic influence, as opposed to assuming personal responsibility and using biblical common sense, places the ministry of deliverance under suspicion in the minds of many. I've heard completely irresponsible statements from people in this camp, and you probably have too. If, for example, someone treats his or her spouse like dirt and is overcontrolling with the kids, that person doesn't have to look very far to find out why his or her mate isn't very responsive and the kids are rebellious. Yet this person can sit down with you over coffee and say, "It's demonic, man. Spiritual warfare. It's tearing my house apart." I'm tempted to say, "Well, there may be some demonic influence, but I don't think it's your spouse or your kids. I think maybe you're deceived." When someone spiritualizes everything into the demonic realm, those of us just going through life and dealing with our issues responsibly don't want to be that out of touch with reality, and we begin to think that every mention of demonic influence is pretense. We don't want to be characterized that way, so we question the validity of any ministry of deliverance.

That's why it is extremely important to stick to Scripture. A lot of questions come up with this type of ministry—whether demons can influence the weather, whether generational curses are real, and all that sort of speculation—and some people who practice deliverance have very specific answers to some of these questions. If you ask them how they know, you'll find that much of their information comes from interviewing demons during an exorcism. I have a hard time accepting information from "the father of lies" and his operatives. I can't put too much stock in what they say. Maybe their answers are right, but I don't have any biblical references for some of them. All I know is that if I stick with Scripture, I'll always stay on track. I'll avoid extremes, I won't be out of touch with reality, and I won't become obsessed with the demonic influences in my life. I'll know what is spiritual conflict and what isn't, and I'll be able to deal with issues appropriately.

## The Causes of Demonic Influence

There are levels of demonic influence. Oppression is a basic, minimal level, and from there it can increase to various levels of harassment, obsession, compulsion, control, and possession.

Michael Pocock of Dallas Seminary shows a continuum of demonic influence in progressive steps of demonization:[13]

opposition→influence→oppression→obsession→control→possession→death

*the normal tendencies of demonization are:*
→ from external to internal
→ from hidden to open attacks
→ increasing control
→ increasing severity

When some people talk about demonic influence, they think in all-or-nothing terms: possession or complete freedom. The Bible doesn't make such a black-and-white distinction; it refers to demonization and demonic influences, and an entire spectrum of intensity can be inferred from scriptural references. A lot of the confusion over these issues arises not from the Bible but from the semantics we use. Personally, I don't believe a Christian can actually be *possessed* by a demon. But there may be levels of influence and control that can simulate those symptoms. The critical thing to understand is not which level of demonic influence people are under, but how they got there.

One pathway to demonic influence is *active seeking*. The question for some people is not whether demons exist but how they can find them and get involved. In Santa Cruz you could sign up for courses on how to cast a spell, find local meetings of warlocks, learn how to channel, and seek out all kinds of other overt participation in the satanic realm. For others, the pathway is very passive—going to see a palm reader while on vacation, playing with a Ouija board, and other such seemingly innocent activities. They get sucked in before they ever realize what they are involved in.

Go to your local music and video store and scan the "dark" titles. Go to a local high school and ask where the Goths, who dress in black and explore the underworld, hang out. For most, it's a clique, a club, a peer group, or a "harmless" foray into the spiritual world. But little do they know the reality of the powers in which they dabble.

*Sin* is probably the most common pathway to demonic influence. For people who consider their sins as personality quirks, emotional issues, or character flaws, that's a harsh statement. We don't usually think of our sin in demonic terms. But Jesus said in John 8:34 that everyone who sins is a slave to sin, and then he goes on to describe his antagonists as children of their father, the devil (v. 44). There's an issue that isn't dealt with, people don't repent of it, they become enslaved to it, and then demonic forces begin to infiltrate their lives on the access roads provided. Sin is an open door to evil spirits. That should be sobering to all of us.

*Spiritual rebellion*—a deliberate willingness to sin—is another cause for demonic influence in a person's life. According to 1 Samuel 15:23, rebellion is like divination or witchcraft. When we know what God wants us to do and we stiff-arm him, refusing his will and choosing to go our own way, we open ourselves up to the original rebels. We make a clear statement that we are like-minded with rebellious spirits that were cast out of heaven for their rejection of God's will.

Deuteronomy 18:10–11 spells out several *occult activities* that are detestable to God and inviting to the enemy. Divination, sorcery, omens, witchcraft, spells, and attempting to contact the dead open pathways for demonic spirits to infiltrate our lives. The issue is not whether séances and astrological predictions are done in a spirit of "innocent fun." A child can strike a match in complete innocence, but a flame still results. The issue with our innocent fun is that these activities do have a supernatural link to the dark forces of this world, and those forces capitalize on our invitations, whether we are aware of them or not.

Avoiding these dangerous activities isn't enough, however. We also need to avoid those who practice them. That doesn't mean that we have to keep them outside the realm of ministry—Jesus died for them too—but we are not to develop friendships with anyone who is involved in occult activity. Paul gives clear instructions about that in 2 Corinthians 6:14–16: light and darkness cannot fellowship together. If we don't want to open our lives to demons, we don't want to open them to the servants of demons either. We should pray for them and minister to them but never fellowship with them.

Probably the most common cause of demonic influence is *unresolved anger and bitterness*. Churches that keep a safe distance from sin, rebellion, and the occult are often safe havens for the bitter and resentful. Many Christians are not aware that unresolved anger is an open door to demonic hosts. Ephesians 4:26–27 is very explicit about how anger that isn't handled quickly gives the devil a foothold. Unforgiveness and unresolved conflict have devastating results, not the least of which is easy exploitation by the enemy.

I once counseled a family who looked squeaky clean, moral, and biblical on the surface, except for the black eye that the wife wore. Underneath the surface there were multiple sources of bitterness between husband and wife, and his bitterness often resulted in fits of rage and uncontrollable, violent outbursts. After some special sessions of counseling, I noticed a repeated theme: "He's a wonderful husband most of the time, but certain things set him off, and it's like he becomes a different person." I had counseled others in abusive situations before, but the dynamics of this situation seemed clearly demonic. It was especially intense and volatile, and the result was tragic. The underlying sins were never dealt with, the belt of truth was never applied, and the foothold of the enemy remained strong. Little did either husband or wife know that their unresolved anger had opened the door for significant demonic infiltration.

## New Testament Evidences of Demonic Influence

How do you know if something is demonic? We are complicated beings with physical, psychological, and spiritual components. It isn't always easy to get to the bottom of a problem or a conflict. We must make sure we carefully evaluate all of the physical factors and sift through emotional issues; but sometimes the spiritual overlaps in a way that doesn't allow for purely medical or psychological explanations. Our issues are easily traceable to the logical progression of things: we're stressed because we haven't gotten enough sleep, or we're in conflict because of clearly dysfunctional relationships. But it isn't always that simple. Sometimes we need to ask if the enemy is at work behind the scenes of our lives.

In the New Testament, God has given us plenty of examples of Satan at work. There are Old Testament examples too—Saul was driven mad by the demonic influences in which he dabbled, and Job's crisis was instigated by Satan's work—but the preponderance of examples applicable to the church today are found in New Testament accounts. These examples don't necessarily imply that demonic influence is always involved, but they do indicate the areas in which demonic influence *can* be involved. They are much like symptoms that a doctor observes—he knows several conditions that can cause such symptoms, but he has to narrow it down to the true source. The Bible doesn't imply that all of the following symptoms are demonic, but it does warn us to consider the demonic as a possible source.

- *Severe sickness* (Matt. 12:22)—Obviously, not all sickness is demonic, but there are some kinds that are untreatable by conventional wisdom or medicine. If you encounter a bizarre, complicated sickness that has not responded to treatment, it is at least possible, according to Scripture, that there is some demonic source behind it. We consider diet, physical conditioning, exposure to toxins, and many other factors in diagnosing a disease. It may be worthwhile on some occasions to also examine the spiritual factors that may be behind it. On a few rare occasions, I've met with people who have exhausted every medical option and have discovered demonic influence as the source of their sickness. Intensive spiritual warfare prayer in those cases does provide the cure for the spiritual source of their problem.
- *Divination* (Acts 16:16)—Not all fortune-tellers are fakes. Some have a genuine ability to divine the future. Those who are con artists are just that; those who aren't con artists receive their abilities from demons. Avoid them all. If you have ever dabbled in trying to tell the future, whether through seemingly innocent board games, tarot cards, or any other such practice, it's important to consider whether any current problems are a result of a demonic influence you may have invited into your life at that time.
- *Unusual physical strength* (Mark 5:2–3)—Once while I was preaching, a man started walking aggressively up the aisle. At first we thought he was drunk, but his eyes were bulging and he was able to shake off whoever tried to hold him. It took three or four people to get him under control. He had unusual strength, which is a common symptom of demonization.
- *Fits of rage* (Mark 5:4)—Uncontrollable, irrepressible rage that surpasses a normal emotional reaction can be caused by demonic influence.
- *Split personality* (Mark 5:6–7)—We had a woman with multiple personalities in our congregation once, and no one could get a handle on exactly who she was. It confused our leadership team at first. One group of people would characterize her one way, and others would counter that she wasn't like that at all. Everyone seemed to have a different experience with her. Eventually we discovered that she had more than one personality and that she could switch in an instant. Then we found out that she had done quite a bit of dab-

bling in the occult and there was a tremendous amount of demonic influence going on. Her split personality was the result. Deliverance came only when her excellent medical and psychological treatment was undergirded with specific deliverance ministry.

- *Resistance to spiritual help* (Mark 5:7)—Most people who have serious problems welcome any help they can get. People who have an immediate negative reaction to spiritual help may be manifesting demonic resistance to the power of God. The gospel is a threat to them just as light is to darkness. This was really apparent to me during a funeral for a teenage victim of a heroin overdose. Our auditorium was filled, and two-thirds of the people were dressed in gothic clothes and makeup. It was the most evil sense I've ever felt in a church. Many of this young man's friends who spoke at the funeral talked about the darkness of death and how they didn't want to die. But during my message, as soon as the name of Jesus was mentioned, many of them pushed back in their chairs. A lot of them even got up and left. God did an amazing work there, as many received Christ and were freed. I have never seen such a clear illustration of light pushing back darkness and of the resistance that people under demonic influence have to the message of life they acknowledge that they crave.
- *Other voices from within* (Mark 5:9)—People frequently tell me their experiences of hearing multiple voices that contradict God and his Word or that cast a certain situation into confusion and darkness. Audible (or nearly audible) voices that don't line up with God's Word and the clear teaching of Scripture can be demonic manifestations.
- *Occult powers* (Deut. 18:10–11)—Anything that fits into the categories of witchcraft, sorcery, spells, omens, mediums, spiritists, divination, or other supernatural contact outside of Christ is a clear indication of demonic influence.

### In Your Life

- Has this chapter helped you become more sensitive to demonic influences in your surroundings? If so, how?
- How might you be able to use your discernment of demonization in your relationships, your church, and your city?

# 15

# How to Find Freedom

Long my imprisoned spirit lay, fast bound in sin and nature's night. Thine eye diffused a quickening ray, I woke, the dungeon flamed with light. My chains fell off, my heart was free, I rose, went forth, and followed Thee.

Charles Wesley

Within the first couple of years in Santa Cruz, my education in spiritual warfare moved to the graduate level. A very calm and quiet man in his twenties came to me one day and shared some struggles he was having in his life. He talked about voices he was hearing and terrible thoughts that were coming into his mind. He had been in counseling and had tried to work through the emotional and psychological issues as well as the counselors could help him. After a number of meetings with me and another pastor, it became evident that he had been exposed to and had dabbled in the occult and that what we were seeing seemed to be some level of demonization.

I didn't know what we were in for. My fellow pastor had a good grasp of Scripture and had done significantly more spiritual warfare than I had, having been a pastor in the Santa Cruz area for some time. We scheduled a day to meet with this young man and address the spiritual issues in his life. We went "prayed up" and spent a substantial amount of time going through the ways to confront demonic spirits and the steps of deliverance. As we did, I had my first experience hearing another voice come out of a human being. It was a strange-sounding, angry growl that resisted us as we confronted the evil spirits in the man's life. We repeatedly claimed our position in Christ and ordered the demonic spirits to depart, spending the better part of two hours in intense warfare, all while voices responded in hostility to our commands.

I don't mind admitting that I was shocked—and scared to death—at this experience of frontline spiritual warfare. Yet God honors his Word. The ways in which we ministered to that young man came straight from God's provision of tools, resources, and spiritual power for us as believers to confront the invisible world. We experienced victory in this situation, just as God promised.

## The Cure for Demonic Influence

Demonic influence is not a foreign concept for many Christians. I've had people line up after I've taught on this subject and tell me that these biblical principles confirm what they already suspected. Many people have already discerned that there is some level of demonic influence in their life or in the lives of people they know, either internally or in some external situation. But diagnosing the problem is just the first step. The biggest question most people have is what to do about it.

First, make sure your general understanding of the gospel is solid. Victory is always through the cross of Christ. Colossians 2:15 is an encouraging statement of that fact. Review it as often as necessary. Jesus disarmed the powers and authorities and made a public spectacle of them in his triumph at the cross. Remember also that victory is in the name of Christ (Matt. 10:1; Acts 5:16). The disciples and the early church experienced the power of Jesus's name regularly. In addition, understand that victory is by the power of the Holy Spirit. Greater is the one who dwells in you than the one who has infiltrated and corrupted this world (1 John 4:4). Being well grounded in the power of the cross, the name of Jesus, and the Holy Spirit is a prerequisite for all attempts to overcome the enemy.

As you read the steps for deliverance in the next few pages, think through your relationship network and your own personal experiences. You may have already discovered that demonic influence might be at the core of some problem in your life or in the lives of people you know and love. I want you to take a deep breath and ask yourself this question: "Does God want me to be the point person in this situation to help bring deliverance?" If the answer is *yes* in any situation you know of, you need to carefully consider the specific steps that can bring Jesus's power and authority into a spiritual conflict.

## Biblical Steps to Deliverance

### 1. Accept Christ

The first step is obvious. Accept Christ as Savior. John 1:12 says that those who receive Jesus have been given the right to become children of God. You may have started reading this book at the urging of a friend or relative but without seeing through the lens of a relationship with Christ. If so, you probably approached the material with some level of suspicion. If, somewhere along the way, God has been speaking to you and putting some real-life conflict into perspective, you may be tempted to enter the fight right away. But if you have never accepted Jesus as your Savior, you do not have the protection of the Holy Spirit. Trying to battle demonic spirits on your own would be a terrible mistake. The first thing you need to do is admit that you need a Savior, believe that when Jesus died on the cross he paid for your sins, and have a change of mind about your old life and turn away from it—which is what *repent* means. The moment you do that, Jesus will come into your life, you'll be sealed with his Spirit, and you'll be transferred from the kingdom of darkness to the kingdom of light. That is the prerequisite to any engagement in battle.

### 2. Repent of Known Sin

If you're a believer, however, the next step is to make sure you have repented of any sinful pattern that has emerged in your life (1 John 1:9). I've heard confessions from people addicted to a sinful habit that no one would suspect of them, and only when they saw startling works of the enemy erupt in their lives did they realize the gravity of their sin. Confession and repentance are extremely important. Whether your habit is lust, pornography, alcohol, drugs, compulsive shopping, food, greed, or anything else that is controlling your life, deal with it. Agree with God about your sin and then trust in the promise of 1 John 1:9 that if you confess your sin, God is faithful and just to forgive your sin and cleanse you of all unrighteousness.

Human beings are often deceived about our addictions and compulsions, believing that we can soothe and satisfy our deep spiritual issues. Even for Christians, it's hard to identify our false props and face up to them. When was the last time, for example, that you were with a group of Christians in a Bible study or fellowship and heard someone ask God to forgive his or her materialism? It's the sacred cow of the Western church, even though Scripture is very clear that the deceitfulness of riches and the desire for "stuff" can choke the truth of God's Word in an otherwise fertile heart. We've got all sorts of critical needs around the world as well as plenty of churches and missionaries desperate for financial support. And Satan has the majority of evangelicals hoodwinked into believing that material things will satisfy them. Various sources indicate that something like less than 4 percent of born-again believers give even a tithe—10 percent of their income. That means that 96 percent of Christians in one of history's most prosperous countries have abundant resources at hand but have been deluded into giving God a small tip.

Think about that. Most Christians are much more committed to giving a waitress a 15 percent tip after a meal than to giving God a tenth of their income after he saved them from eternal despair. When was the last time you finished a meal at a restaurant and said to your spouse, "I know the service was good, but let's just blow them off this time"? Or worse yet, embarrassed your server by giving a one-dollar tip on the table after a fifty-dollar meal? Millions of Christians do that with God.

Weird, demonic manifestations in the middle of the night aren't a necessary precondition for deliverance. If someone has been deceived by the lies of the enemy—whether through materialism or any other sin—that person is rendered inoperative. If that's your situation, the remedy is to confess. God isn't down on you; he loves you. He just knows that you're missing out on an enormous blessing, and so is the kingdom.

## 3. Renounce the Works of the Devil

The third step to deliverance is to renounce the works of the devil (2 Cor. 4:2). If you realize you've been deluded and the Word is being choked out of your life, face up to it and reject the delusion. Turn your back on it. Add to your repentance a clear, emphatic repudiation of what the enemy has already done.

I recently had the privilege of teaching a seminar at the Billy Graham Leadership Training Center in North Carolina. The topic was the attributes of God, and a young woman stopped me after the last session and said, "You keep mentioning this 'lordship of Christ' concept. It keeps ringing in my mind, and I need to know what that means and how to do it." After talking for some time, it was obvious that she was a genuine believer but had never made a complete and clean break with her past, allowing Jesus to be the Lord, CEO, and Master of her life. To fight or confront the enemy prior to this clear break with the past and our allegiance to the Lord is futile.

## 4. Destroy Occult Objects

The fourth step is to destroy occult objects (2 Chron. 14:2–5; 23:17; Acts 19:17–20). If you've dabbled in astrology, used a Ouija board, or participated in some other seemingly harmless activity, destroy whatever evidence you still have. You'll be following the example of the Ephesians who had accepted Christ; those who had been involved in occult practices came together to burn all their scrolls publicly (Acts 19:19). It's not only the practice of occultism that gives the enemy a pathway, it's also the possession of its tools. Distance yourself as far as you can from these things and from the temptation they represent.

## 5. Break Unholy Friendships

The fifth step is to break friendships with people in the occult (2 Cor. 6:14–16). Missionaries often feel the need to befriend occult practitioners as part of their ministry, but there's a way to do that without fellowshipping with evil. Pray, build relationships on neutral turf, find out what's going on in their lives, but do not hang around with people who are immersed in evil practices. Like a doctor who wears gloves and a mask to deal with highly contagious patients, maintain a healthy separation from supernatural evil.

I will never forget a young staff member's experience of sharing Christ in the home of a witch. He came into my office and described drawn curtains, no light, an oppressive atmosphere, and his joy in the midst of it all as he and his team shared Christ's love. Then with a sense of sobriety he said, "I'd never want to go there alone or without a lot of prayer first." His caution is a word of wisdom to us all.

## 6. Rest in Christ's Deliverance

Once you have covered the first five steps, rest in Christ's deliverance (Col. 1:13). Renew your mind to the point that you are able to clearly understand and depend on the safety found in Jesus. Following the steps up to this point is essential, but it won't make the enemy go away. He puts up a fight. Scripture teaches that when a demon is cast out, he goes and gets his most wicked cohorts and returns with a vengeance—*unless* truth and focus took his place when he left. The house has to be put in order before demonic spirits will leave it alone.

## 7. Resist the Devil

The next step is to resist the devil. James 4:1–10 lays it out clearly for us. It is a complete picture of New Testament repentance and resistance. First, submit to God (v. 7). Any area of your life that is not submitted to God in your behavior and your thinking must come under his authority. The flip side of submitting to God is resisting the devil. Insist that you're not going to fall for his schemes anymore. Turn away from whatever activity or false belief you once practiced or held. Then "draw near to God and He will draw near to you" (v. 8). As he draws near, he begins to deal with the issues in your life. But you have to deal with them too: "Cleanse your hands, you sinners," James writes. Whatever tangible activities that came as a result of your sin, stop them. "Purify your hearts, you double-minded" (v. 8). What internal attitudes, lusts, and lies do you need to deal with? We like to think we can have it both ways: submit to the kingdom of God and dabble in the kingdoms of this world. We can't. That's double-mindedness, and it needs to be purified from us.

Then there's an appropriate emotional response: grieve, mourn, and wail (v. 9). Realize that the enemy has captured you, and the King and Redeemer you've been keeping at arm's length has borne the pain of your resistance. Come to him broken. But don't stop there; move on to the promise that follows. Jesus told his disciples that those who mourn are blessed (Matt. 5:4), and here's why: if you humble yourself before the Lord, he will lift you up (James 4:10). God is always near to the brokenhearted, and he saves those who are crushed in spirit.

The temptation for many of us at this point is to think that our sin is too big and beyond hope. If that's where you are, think about David. He really blew it. He committed adultery and murder within a year. It doesn't get much worse than that. At the end of his prayer of repentance, here's what he said: "You do not delight in sacrifice, otherwise I would give it. . . . The sacrifices of God are a broken spirit; a broken and a contrite heart, O God, You will not despise" (Ps. 51:16–17).

The moment you come to God with a broken and contrite heart, God will rush to you. You'll read the parable of the prodigal son (Luke 15:11–32) with new eyes. The Father has been watching and waiting, and when his son returns, he runs to embrace him. There are no crossed arms and raised eyebrows, no lingering resentment. He'll throw a party.

## 8. Renew Your Mind

The next step is to renew your mind by meditating on and applying the Word of God (Matt. 4:4, 7, 10; Eph. 6:17). Fill your mind with good things. Go on a media fast and turn off the TV for a few days. See if you can read through the New Testament in two or three weeks. Many Christians who can read five-hundred-page novels are shocked at the idea of reading through the New Testament. I knew a pastor in San Francisco who read it every single week. He didn't linger in many passages, of course, but he was always able to do it in about a day and a half. As a result, the breadth and depth of his life and character were amazing. Not everyone can do that every week, but it does illustrate that it can be done much more easily than we think. Read and begin a Scripture memory program. Review verses for a couple of minutes before you go to bed and when you first get up. Consider reviewing the executive summaries in this book and memorizing key verses concerning spiritual warfare. Think about them throughout the day. Whatever it takes, let your mind be renewed.

## 9. Pray with Others

Then engage in corporate prayer. You were never called to live the Christian life alone. Almost every New Testament command I can find is in the second-person plural: "you all" do these things. They are corporate instructions, and Jesus himself urged his followers to pray together (Matt. 18:19). People come to me saying they've identified a demonic influence and they've followed all of these steps, and I encourage them to get some key people in their church to come together and pray as a group. There will be times of intense opposition when we need each other. Share your heart, fast if you can, and pray together, first defensively and then offensively. Then see what God will do.

## 10. If Necessary, Exorcise

The final step is exorcism in the name of Jesus (Acts 16:16–18). It usually isn't necessary, but neither should it be a foreign concept to us. Exorcism isn't the domain of horror movies; it's a New Testament practice.

Who should do exorcism? A qualified counselor who is filled with the Holy Spirit, for starters. Ephesians 5:18 and Galatians 5:16 both stress the importance of a Spirit-filled life. Someone who performs an exorcism should have the kind of humility expressed in James 4:7–10, should wear the spiritual armor according to Ephesians 6, should know the Word of God in order to use it as Jesus did in Matthew 4, and should be supported by the prayers of other believers (Matt. 18:19; Eph. 6:18).

You may recall the young man who spoke with a nonhuman voice to a fellow pastor and me or the man who came screaming down the aisle in the middle of one of my sermons. In instances such as these, the demonization is too severe to walk someone through the steps of repentance and separation from occultism. The firmly entrenched spirit needs to be cast out.

That sounds like only a select few should handle such cases, but any Christian clothed in the righteousness of Jesus and filled with the Holy Spirit can do this. There are rare occasions when the situation is really heavy duty and some extensive experience is helpful, and an expert needs to come into the arena. (There are ministries that can help you find someone: those of Neil Anderson and Mark Bubeck, for example.)[14] But the spirit of the New Testament is not that there will be a few gun-slinging professionals performing isolated exorcisms, but that regular, ordinary believers with the badge and authority of Christ can address demonic issues and, when necessary, command demons to leave. It doesn't take a hyperspiritual, highly specialized super-saint; it takes courageous believers who know who they are in Christ, who understand that the foe is formidable but who do not fear him, and who are willing to exercise the power and authority of Christ under the grace and armor of God. When you come against demonic powers in the name of Jesus, they must flee.

## Personal Application: What about You?

Knowing the power of Christ in this battle doesn't mean things are going to be real easy, and it doesn't mean you'll never have a bizarre, frightening experience. As I mentioned earlier, that first experience in my bedroom at night almost scared me to death. Sometimes I would wake up with one of those experiences and have other family members going through the same thing at the same time. But our safety in Christ was beautifully illustrated one night when I got up to get a glass of water.

It was after midnight, and I heard something from my youngest son's bedroom. I felt compelled to check out the sounds coming from my child's bedroom just to make sure he was okay, so I tiptoed over to the door. It was cracked open, and the light from the bathroom allowed me to get a glimpse of what was going on. My ten-year-old son was kneeling by his bed, saying, "Dear Lord Jesus, I thank you that I am complete in Christ, and I thank you that I have the armor of God. Dear Lord, these spirits are seeking to assault me tonight, and in the blood of Jesus, by his great name and power, I command them to leave me alone. I claim right now that greater is he who is in me than he who is in the world. Depart from this bedroom and go where Jesus sends you. Amen." Then I watched him pull back his covers, get in his bed, roll over, and go to sleep.

The next morning at the breakfast table, he said, "You know, dad, I had one of those things happen last night." I played dumb. "Really? What happened?" He simply explained, "Well, I just did spiritual warfare like we talked about."

Now if a ten-year-old with a spiritual Colt .45 and the authority of Jesus can tell demonic spirits what to do and when to do it, don't you think regular people like us—in a balanced, reasoned, and wise approach—can do exactly what God wants us to do? I think so.

## In Your Life

- Have you identified any areas in your life in which you suspect demonic influence? If so, what causes have you been able to discern? Have you taken any steps to break from the source?
- Have you identified any areas in your relational network that are under demonic influence? If so, how might God want you to be involved in the solution?
- How open are the people around you to discussing things like demonization and deliverance? How do their attitudes affect yours? Are you able to openly confess and renounce the works of the enemy with each other?
- In what ways can you help create a climate of openness with spiritual warfare issues among the members of your church?
- What are you currently doing to renew your mind? Is it enough? If not, what specific steps can you take to immerse yourself more in God's Word?

## What You Need to Remember

There are several steps you can take to bring your life into conformity with Scripture on the matter of prayer and deliverance.

1. Assess the quantity and quality of your prayer life. Is it everything both you and God want it to be? If not,
   a. At the beginning of your normal prayer time, make two requests of God: "Today, lay on my heart the issues that you want me to pray for until you are ready for me to stop," and, "In the next few days, impress upon me how my prayer life should change from what it is now."
   b. Then be sensitive to the ways in which God might be leading you. Ask for his guidance until you are convinced you have received it.
2. Pray through the ACTS model (Adoration, Confession, Thanksgiving, Supplication) to make sure your prayers are well-rounded.
3. Ask God to make you spiritually sensitive to demonic influence and to give you wisdom as you seek to discover your role in a specific need for deliverance.

Be persistent in these prayers. God wants you to understand this subject as much as you do—actually, more than you do. Pray earnestly and constantly for the understanding he wants you to have.

# Conclusion

## A Tale of Two Warriors

It started well for Saul. He was anointed king, promised the power of God, and given great victories in God's name. He even demonstrated humility, mercy, and wisdom. But early in his reign, Saul strayed. His impatience on the verge of a battle caused him to take his eyes off of God's clear command. A rash oath brought trouble to his son and his country. His tendency to adapt God's instructions to suit his own desires led to God's rejection of him.

A reign that began in glory ended in disaster. Why? Because the warrior Saul clothed himself in the king's armor before every battle, but he did not guard his heart and his mind. He neglected the spiritual armor of a greater King.

Though Ephesians 6 was written roughly a thousand years after Saul's reign, the principles should have been obvious to an anointed servant of God. But Saul allowed himself to fall victim to sin and rebellion, first by small steps of unbelief and then by enormous leaps of disobedience. A careful reading of Saul's story in 1 Samuel 9–31 shows the sad progression of an armorless warrior.

If the belt of truth is honesty before God and men, Saul had no place to tuck in his robe and attach his armor. After a battle against the Amalekites, before which God had told Saul to destroy *everything* among them, Saul boldly told Samuel the priest that he had carried out the Lord's instructions—in spite of the fact that the Amalekites' livestock was grazing nearby and their king still lived (1 Sam. 15). Saul's integrity was never anchored to absolutes.

If the breastplate of righteousness is understanding God's forgiveness and living according to God's character, Saul's heart was unprotected. He rejected God's true assessment of his sin and listened to the voices of accusing, tormenting spirits. His repentance was always superficial, and he always attempted self-justification before asking God's forgiveness. Righteousness was on his lips, not over his heart.

If the footwear of the gospel of peace is being firmly planted in the mercy of God, Saul was on slippery ground. He was often unmerciful—his jealousy led him on a passionate pursuit to kill David, and he even once hurled a spear at his own son. He demonstrated again and again that he was neither accepting of grace nor willing to grant it. He did not know God's peace.

If the shield of faith is believing God instead of the lies of the enemy, Saul was wounded often. His disobedience seemed minor at first—he simply let himself be intimidated by the taunts of Goliath rather than being zealous for the reputation of God—but his deception progressed rapidly. In the last stages of his tormented life, he even sought out a medium's guidance in place of God's (1 Sam. 28). He went from being afraid of the people to being terrified of the Almighty. He was consumed with fear, not rooted in faith.

If the helmet of salvation is a pure thought life, Saul exposed himself to fatal blows. He was eaten up by his own rationalizing, fear, jealousy, rage, bitterness, and paranoia. Evil spirits tormented his thinking with twisted lies and destructive impulses. His mind was a brutal battlefield, and he was on the losing side.

If the sword of the Spirit is the Word of God, Saul was defenseless. In his early years, when he acted on God's Word, he won battles. After he had rejected God's Word, his attacks resulted in disaster. Instead of wielding his weapons for the sake of his people, he began wielding them for the sake of his own sense of vengeance. In the end, spiritually and physically, Saul ended up dead on the battlefield. And not coincidentally, he was stripped of his armor.

Saul's successor, however, was a different kind of warrior. Like Saul, David displayed humility, mercy, and wisdom in his early years. Unlike Saul, David protected himself with the spiritual armor of God.

David fastened on the belt of truth. When Nathan confronted him about his sin with Bathsheba, David repented immediately, confessing his transgression before men and, in Psalm 51, before God. After demonstrating faithlessness by numbering the troops of Israel, David repented and asked that judgment fall on him, not the nation. David was honest—brutally, painfully honest—with God.

David wore a breastplate of righteousness. God described David as a man after God's heart (1 Sam. 13:14), and he described himself as a God after David's heart (1 Sam. 16:7). A heart linked with God's heart is protected by an impenetrable breastplate. It cannot be fatally wounded.

David had his feet firmly planted in the gospel of peace. In mercy, he spared an unprotected Saul, not once but twice. In mercy, he adopted the last remaining survivor of Saul's once-threatening household. In mercy, he heard Abigail's plea to spare her treacherous husband, who had refused hospitality to David's men. In mercy, he pleaded for the life of a rebellious son. David knew forgiveness, and he shared it with everyone who would accept it.

David gripped the shield of faith. He refused to be intimidated by Goliath's taunts. He even refused Saul's armor before going up against the giant. He walked onto the battlefield armed with only a slingshot and a gigantic confidence in God. And the spear of the enemy never hit its mark.

David wore the helmet of salvation. He immersed his mind in God's wisdom. When God delivered him from Saul, David reaffirmed his allegiance to God's decrees as the key to God's favor (Ps. 18:22). He meditated on God's Word early and often. His mind was saturated with truth.

David wielded the sword of the Spirit. He not only knew the truth, he applied it. When praying about the building of the temple, he reminded God of his promises. When the Philistines seized him, he praised God for his promise of deliverance. David boldly confronted the enemies of God because he had the promises of God to back him up. He fought with a mighty sword, and he died in honor.

David and Saul were not complete opposites, at least not at first. Neither one of them was perfect, but both had the qualities of a king. What made the difference? Over time, one warrior fought according to God's principles, in God's way, in God's timing, and for God's glory. He wore impenetrable spiritual armor, even in his failures. The other warrior fought according to his own principles, his ways, his timing, and for his glory. He left himself unprotected in the most serious way. He shed the armor of God.

The lives of these two men are an apt illustration of the importance of understanding our battles. They remind us that while the war is invisible, victory and defeat are not. How we fight, and what we wear spiritually as we do, will sooner or later show up in real lives and in real ways. The preparation for and the execution of our battles today can determine the course of our lives and those of future generations.

I urge you, then, as a matter of utmost importance, to be strong in the Lord. Stand firm and be alert. Gird yourself and use your weapons. Above all, pray. You represent the greatest army in all of history, and you fight for the greatest of causes. When the King comes in victory, you will receive the honors of a valiant warrior. And the invisible war will never need to be fought again.

# Notes

1. Francis Schaeffer, *True Spirituality* (Wheaton: Tyndale, 1971).

2. C. S. Lewis, *The Screwtape Letters* (New York: Macmillan, 1982), 33.

3. Kenneth S. Wuest, *Word Studies in the Greek New Testament*, vol. 1 (Grand Rapids: Eerdmans, 1973), 143.

4. Ibid.

5. Ibid., 144.

6. Ibid.

7. A. W. Tozer, *Knowledge of the Holy* (San Francisco: HarperSanFrancisco, 1961), 82.

8. S. D. Gordon, *Quiet Talks on Prayer* (New York: Grosset & Dunlop, 1941), 12–13.

9. Elisabeth Elliot, *Love Has a Price Tag* (Ventura, CA: Regal Books, 2005), 127–29.

10. Warren Wiersbe, *Be Rich* (Wheaton: Victor, 1976), 172.

11. Gordon, *Quiet Talks on Prayer*, 12–13.

12. Mark Bubeck, *The Adversary* (Chicago: Moody Press, 1975); Mark Bubeck, *Overcoming the Adversary* (Chicago: Moody Press, 1984); Neil Anderson, *The Bondage Breaker* (Eugene, OR: Harvest House Publishers, 2000); Neil Anderson, *Victory over the Darkness* (Ventura, CA: Gospel Light, 2000).

13. Chart from notes taken at a pastors' conference in October 1992. Michael Pocock is chair and senior professor of world missions and intercultural studies, Dallas Theological Seminary.

14. Neil Anderson and Mark Bubeck, www.ficm.org (Freedom in Christ Ministries).

**Chip Ingram** is the president and teaching pastor for Living on the Edge, an international teaching and discipleship ministry. His passion is to help everyday Christians actually "live like Christians" by raising the bar of discipleship. A pastor for over twenty years, Chip has a unique ability to communicate truth and winsomely challenge people to live out their faith. Chip is the author of nine books, including *Good to Great in God's Eyes*; *Love, Sex & Lasting Relationships*; *God: As He Longs for You to See Him*; and *The Invisible War*. Chip and his wife, Theresa, have four children and six grandchildren.

For more information about Chip Ingram or Living on the Edge, please visit www.LivingOnTheEdge.org

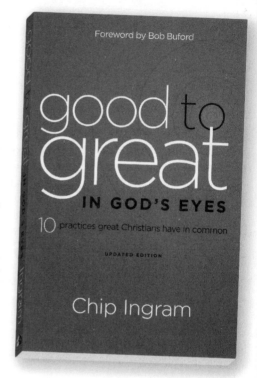